The Internet Marketing Digest

The Internet Marketing Digest

Discover How To Market Any Product or
Service Online and Offline for Pennies
Using Proven Time Tested Methods

Bob Brolhorst

Writer's Showcase
San Jose New York Lincoln Shanghai

The Internet Marketing Digest
Discover How To Market Any Product or Service Online and Offline for Pennies Using Proven Time Tested Methods

Writer's Showcase
an imprint of iUniverse.com, Inc.

For information address:
iUniverse.com, Inc.
5220 S 16th, Ste. 200
Lincoln, NE 68512
www.iuniverse.com

ISBN: 0-595-19053-7

Printed in the United States of America

This book is dedicated to my wife Brenda for being so understanding for all the hours that I spent away from her to try to do all the research it took to put this book together. To Jeremy , Brandon, and Paige my three children who I love dearly.

Contents

To LaDonna Wieland for helping me get the book setup for print without her I would have been lost.

Introduction

I want to personally thank you for purchasing one of the world's best Internet Business Books available. I would like to take the time to make sure that you use this book to its fullest potential. If you take each chapter and apply them to your particular business you will see an increase in your total profits, that in your wildest dreams you couldn't imagine happening. The procedures in this book have been tested over and over again to insure that what you will learn does work, not just for one business, but for all businesses on the Internet.

It will take time to use everything that is listed in this book. Don't think that you have to use everything in a day, or week, or month. It takes time and hard work to build a profitable business. Some of the information you can start using today and see results in a couple of days. Some of the other information may take a little while longer before you see any results.

To best utilize this home book let me start by giving you some reasons why you should have your business on the Internet. There are over 1.5 million web pages born daily. So you can't say that there aren't enough people on the Internet to justify putting your business on the World Wide Web. The Internet doubles in size every 8 months. 50 % of all the web traffic goes to the 900 Websites currently listed in the top of their prospective business categories. Even though these numbers seem staggering, the Internet is still in its infancy. If you compared it to a glass of water it equals just a teaspoon full within the glass.

Just to give you an idea of what you will be in store for by expanding or targeting your home-based business on the Internet. The average home-based business earns $50,250 per year. This is almost double of the $26,000 that the average United States employee earns. About 20% of all home-based businesses owners are making in excess of $75,000 per year. Source: Entrepreneur Magazine.

It is also projected that by the year 2002 that 60% of all U.S. businesses will be home-based businesses. Of the 55 million people that are currently o the Internet, that figure will increase to over 300 million by the year 2002. The number of people working from home jumped a whopping 56% from 1980 to 1990. Source: U.S. Census Bureau.

Keep this course at your fingertips and refer to it often. It can benefit you years down the road. Some of the information will change due to new technology. But most of what's in this course has stood the test of time and still works today. It will continue to work 50 years from now. If you ever have any questions be sure and drop me e-mail at *bbrolhorst@wave5marketing.com* and I will get back to you either by e-mail or if need be by personal phone call. (Just leave your phone number and a good time to call.)

After you have read over the entire course, start over and read it again. You may have overlooked some important items. Even if you apply just a few of the marketing techniques you will see a sizable increase in your profits.

There is no better time to start a home-based business or expand your existing business to the Internet. I now invite you to share in my success and know how. I have divided up this course into an easy to use format. Take a moment to see for yourself. The abundance of tools, services, and techniques, you will discover is well worth the look. Remember this course comes with a full 100% 1-Year money back guarantee. If you are not totally satisfied I will gladly refund your money. No questions asked. Enjoy the tour.

Now lets get started. Go to chapter 1 and I will begin guiding you through the many aspects of working on the Internet, from choosing a server, to building your Website, promoting your business either online or off-line, and much, much more.

Chapter 1

How to Pick an Internet Service Provider

"You win more friends in life by being interested in others than trying to get others interested in you".

—Dale Carnegie

Many people that are new to the Internet need to know the difference between an Internet Service Provider (ISP) and a Web hosting Service, before setting up a Website and putting it out on the World Wide Web. Just as an example, one of my local ISP's here in Lincoln, Nebraska, is a company called Navix. This is offered through my local telephone company, as are most local ISP's. Now, Navix will get me connected to the "WWW" where I can visit various Chat rooms or "discussion groups" and "news groups" or local bulletin boards (BBS).

Some of these ISP's do offer you space on their servers where you can place your Website. As with so many other requirements to your business, especially in this case, leave the web hosting to the professionals. What do I mean by this? Companies like Accesspoint, Mind Spring, Netcom, or Gen. are experts and have the equipment to make sure your Website is available close to 100% of the time 365 days of the year. A lot of Internet Service Providers cannot guarantee this.

Now if I want to go to Chat rooms, then the ISP's in my opinion, far out weigh what Web hosting can do for you, so you see that they are both equally important, but they each have their place. I am connected with America Online (AOL) I use primarily for discussion groups and to find free Information. I also use Accesspoint for primarily uploading the Web Pages and Sites that I design, and for the web browser so I may access any URL from here. AOL servers seem to be down more than Accesspoint, so if I want people to access my Website I prefer for them. Nothing is more embarrassing and unprofessional than to give someone your Website address and to have him or her to come back and tell you they could not access it. So it is very important to have a Web hosting servers are up at least 98% of the time, if not you stand to lose substantial income.

ACCESS POINT #1 WEB HOSTING AND E —COMMERCE PROVIDER

Access Point Is One Of The Top Web Hosting And E – Commerce Providers.
http://www.accesspoint.com

Access Point is a company that helped usher in the age of Internet. As such, it has some unique insight into the technologies and issues around Web hosting. Access Point's services are extremely broad. Virtually every available requirement can be met," reads the review by "The Access Point experience shows in their step-by-step instructions for new hosting users, and pre-defined templates to help new users get up and running quickly. For more experienced users, Access Point offers easy ways to change account levels. Add to all this Access Point's excellent customer support, and it's easy to see why Access Point ranks above the rest of the field."

Access Point has consistently achieved high marks as the ultimate web host provider! Since its inception Access Point has consistently moved ahead of the competiton. Access Point ranks high in each of the five categories: value, quality, support, flexibility and miscellaneous.

Value:

Measured by the amount of features the web Host Company provides for the cost of their services.

Quality:

Measured by the ease, speed and reliability of connectivity and service.

Support:

Measured by early notification of and rate of responsiveness to system problems, updating as to status of problem resolution, and knowledge of technical support staff;

Flexibility:

Measured by ease of construction and manipulation of web site, ability to upgrade and choose between a wide variety of value-added services, timeliness of changes taking effect;

Miscellaneous:

Any aspect of the web host provider not covered by the other categories.

Due to the expertise Access Point offers in the development and support of a full array of web hosting services, as well as the overall ease-of-use and flexibility of their products, they believe their success in web hosting is attributed to responding directly to their customers' needs for scaleable, value-added solutions that allow them to establish and maintain their own distinctive on-line presence."

Access Point web hosting services include individual productivity and business connectivity solutions. Key benefits include: on-line domain name registration, a broad range of disk space options, web authoring tools, multiple mailboxes, backup frequency options, CGI access and web site statistics. These options allow Access Point customers to get on-line, build, maintain, and expand their web presence as their needs grow. Additional information on Access Point's web hosting services can be found at *http://www.accesspoint.com*

What's best for me?

The first step to getting your web pages online, you may need to rent some empty web space. There are three different ways you can do this commercially. From one of the big online companies like CompuServe or the Microsoft Network; one that works all over the nation, like AT&T; or from a small local Internet business in Charlottesville.

If even after reading this article you are nervous about looking into any of these options alone, you may want to hire a Website Designer first to help you with renting space as well as designing your web pages. That is where one of my business associates or I can help, you can contact me at Bob Brolhorst, Wave 5 Marketing -402-423-7607.

One more tidbit, it is quite easy to switch from one rented web space to another if you become dissatisfied. You just have your web pages moved to a new empty space on the web. (If you have gotten a domain name, there'll be a few more things to do—but I'll get to all that later in this article.)

Do I Need a Computer?

It depends, do you just want a Website designer to make your page and update it regularly? Are interested in receiving e-mail from customers or ever viewing your own page? If the answer is no, you don't need a computer. But be prepared for any of the companies below to be very surprised when you tell them. They see themselves as catering to people who want to access the wonderful Internet, not to people who just want web pages and not use the Internet themselves.

But if you want to use the Internet, and plan to make minor or even major changes to your own pages, receive e-mail from customer's etc., you'll need a computer and a modem. What you need, and what you may already have is sufficient, is beyond the scope of this article. My best advice is to hunt hard for someone who knows about such things, such as a consultant, like myself.

America Online and CompuServe both allow you to put Webpages on their web at no additional cost. If you already subscribe to one of these services, or were planning to subscribe, this may be the best way for you to create a web site (and quite possibly the cheapest).

Keep the following drawbacks in mind:

America Online and CompuServe may have tight limits on how many pages and graphics you can put on the web, make sure you aren't going to exceed these limits. Check their latest policies on commercial versus personal web pages before proceeding. America Online custom software for viewing the web is remarkably poor. So I would suggest either Netscape or Internet Explorer. If you happen to sign up with Netcom they have an excellent browser.

In my research of Internet service providers, I have also run a cross a company that seems to offer a lot of features for a small price tag, The Global Entrepreneurs Network. They even offer a guarantee, that is something most Internet Service Providers don't give you. The Exclusive GEN Zero-Risk Guarantee! If you cancel your GEN Membership for any reason during the first 30 days we will cheerfully refund you your entire investment— including your set up fee. YOU HAVE ZERO RISK! Now I don't know whether this is a good solution for you, but I suggest that you check them out *http://home.gen.com/* here are a few things that they offer:

- Cutting Edge Technology—Windows NT based hosting
- Complete Site Transfer—We will move your site for you!
- T3 Speed!
- Uptime Guarantee!
- MB of server space
- Complete Frontpage 98 support
- Unlimited Hits/Traffic
- Unlimited Autoresponders and E-Mail aliases
- Up to 5 POP E-Mail Accounts
- Virtual Domain Support (www.yourdomain.com)
- Live Web Statistics
- hr. network monitoring and support!

Your first year investment: $319.00, including one-time setup fees $50.00 and completes site transfer. Your cost per month:

$21.27! (Monthly cost based on 15 months incl. 3 free months of service. Cost thereafter: $269/year)

America Online   1-800-827-6364
CompuServe   1-800-336-6823

America Online and CompuServe offer access to both their specialized services, as well as to the Internet and Web; other companies specialize in offering only Internet and Web access. They are generally called Internet Service Providers, or ISP's. Some of these companies are national: they offer access from almost anywhere in the U.S. Others are smaller, offering access for only a single region or town—Charlottesville has a handful of these.

If America Online or CompuServe is not for you, which ISP should you go with? Don't forget word of mouth, if anyone you know is satisfied with the service of their ISP, check into it.

Here's A List of Web Hosting Companies

Access Point: http://www.accesspoint.com
AT&T WorldNet: *http://www.att.com/worldnet*
America Online: *http://www.aol.com*
Brigadoon.Com, Inc.: *http://www.brigadoon.com*
CompuServe: *http://www.compuserve.com*
Concentric Network: *http://www.concentric.net/*
DIGEX, Inc.: *http://www.digex.net/*
Delphi Internet Services: *http://www.delphi.com/*
EarthLink Network: *http://www.earthlink.net/*
Epoch Network/HLC: *http://www.hlc.net/*
GTE Internet Solutions: *http://www.get.net/*
IBM Internet Connection: *http://www.ibm.net/*

IDT (International Discount Telecommunications):
http://www.idt.net
InfiNet: *http://www.infi.net/*
MCI Internet 2000: *http://www.mci.com/*
MindSpring: *http://www.mindspring.com/*
Primenet: *http://www.globalcenter.net/*
Prodigy: *http://www.prodigy.com*
SpryNet: *http://www.sprynet.com/*
USA.NET: *http://www.usa.net/*
UUNet Technologies: *http://www.uu.net/*
Whole Earth Networks: *http://www.wenet.net/*
CampusMCI: *http://www.campus.mci.net*

Does the company have Microsoft Frontpage server extensions?

This is only important if you plan to use Frontpage (a very popular Web-authoring program). If the hosting company doesn't have the server extensions installed, some of the Frontpage features won't work.

How Much Does It Cost?

Most services charge a setup fee, and then a monthly charge. Some don't have a setup fee; some will waive the setup fee if you are transferring an existing Web site and domain from another location. Even if they don't advertise, if you are transferring a site ask if they will waive the fee.

Minimum Contract and Guarantee?

Some Web-hosting companies' want you to pay a year's fee at once, you should ask if you could pay for say, three months. Some simply go month by month, others charge by the month and may give the first month free—the ideal situation. Ask what sort of guarantees they offer; some may offer a 30-day money-back guarantee. Get the guarantee in writing, if you can.

How Much Disk Space?

Your Web site will be limited to a certain amount of disk space; you can buy more if needed. Small, low-cost accounts may have just a couple of megabytes of disk space; larger sites will get tens, even hundreds of Megs. You can actually get quite a lot into a megabyte or two, and a really huge site will need only a few hundred Megs.

How much are Hit and Data-Transfer Charges?

Some companies charge you for the number of hits—the number of times someone transfers one of your pages to his browser. Others charge according to the amount of data transferred out of your Web site. Either way, the busier your site, the more you'll be charged under these pricing schedules. Others have no limit. Unlimited use may not be so good if it means that all the sites handled by the server are very busy, of course. In any case, most companies provide a certain minimum data transfer for free, which is usually plenty for most sites.

How much are Upgrades?

If your Web site grows, so will your hosting needs? Check to see how much it'll cost you to add more disk space, transfer more data, create more e-mail accounts, and so on.

How Much to Host Multiple Domain Names?

If you have more than one domain name, you can have them all point to the same Web site. For instance, you might have one domain name for your company and other domain names that you are using to promote specific products. There are different ways to handle this. All the domains can point to the same directory, or you can have separate directories for each domain. Of course, there are different ways to charge, too. You may be allowed two domains for free, perhaps, with an additional fee for extra domains. Or maybe you'll pay an additional fee for all extra domains.

Is there a Charge for E-Mail Accounts?

You'll generally get an e-mail account with your Web site. Sometimes you'll get several accounts even though you may need no more than one. Some companies, however, may charge extra for the account. With a single e-mail account, you can retrieve e-mail that has been sent to various addresses: info@acmesewercover.com, sales@acmesewercover.com, Joe @ acmesewercover.com, Susie @ acmesewercover.com and so on.

How Many Mail Forwarding Accounts?

You may also want to make sure the Web-hosting Company allows you to set up mail forwarding—automatically defining certain types of incoming e-mail messages to be forwarded somewhere else. For instance, messages to Susie @ acmesewer-cover.com could be forwarded to susiesewer@aol.com. Ask how many accounts can be forwarded.

Do You Have Mail Responders?

A mail responder, or **Autoresponders**, is a program that automatically responds to incoming mail. For instance, if someone sends e-mail to info@acmesewercover.com, an informational message can be sent back. These can be very useful, so I recommend that you use a company that provides these. There are several things a good **Autoresponders** should be able to do:

- *Quote the incoming message in the autoresponse*
- *Save the incoming message*
- *Grab the e-mail address from the incoming message and put it in a text file*

The last of these is particularly important, as it allows you to collect e-mail addresses from messages sent to your Autoresponders.

Do You Have Mailing Lists?

A mailing list is a discussion group based on the e-mail system. You may want to set one up—they're very useful promotional tools. Even if you don't want to host a discussion group, you can use a mailing-list program to distribute a newsletter. Many companies have mailing-list software available for their clients to use—if so, ask whether there's an additional cost, how many mailing lists you are allowed to have, and how many members per list.

Do I Get a Shell Account? (Telnet Access)

A shell account allows you to log onto the Web site using Telnet, and modify files and directories. This can be useful, and you'll find that most companies provide a shell account. Some don't, though, and this can present problems. For instance, if you want to install your own CGI scripts (see below), you may need Telnet access so you can get to the scripts and modify their permissions, rename files, and so on.

Do I Get FTP Access?

You'll need FTP (File Transfer Protocol) access. This allows you to transfer files to and from your Web site, so virtually all companies provide this service. Some may provide a different way to transfer files, such as using Frontpage. But even if you use Frontpage, it's nice to have FTP access too.

Can I set Up an Anonymous FTP Site?

This is not the same as FTP accesses to your Web site. Rather, it allows you to set up an FTP site that people can access to download files.

You might want to do this if you are distributing software, for instance. While it's possible to transfer files directly from your Web site, it's sometimes handy to have an FTP site, too. Anyone without good Web access can still use the FTP site. Some FTP sites can resume interrupted downloads; say someone tries to transfer a file, gets halfway through, and his ISP or phone company drops the line, he may be able to come back and continue the transfer where he left off—a very handy feature for large downloads.

Do You Have a Secure Server?

If you plan to take orders on-line or transfer sensitive information, you'll need a secure server (you'll often see it referred to as an SSL server, meaning a Secure Sockets Layer server). For instance, credit-card information typed into a form will be encrypted before being sent from the user's Web browser to the server. There may be an additional fee to use the secure server.

You don't have to have a secure server to take orders on-line, but many people won't place orders without it.

Do You Have Shopping-Cart Software?

If you plan to sell products and want to offer users some kind of catalog combined with an order form, you might want to find out if the Web-hosting company has any shopping-cart software already available and, if so, it's capabilities and cost. If not, ask if you can add your own.

Can I Use CGI Scripts?

CGI means Common Gateway Interface. It's a way to provide interactively to Web pages, in particular to handle the input from forms. For instance, you can use CGI to take information from a form and send it to your e-mail account, and many shopping-cart programs use CGIs.

Many Web-hosting companies have libraries of CGI scripts you can use. Some allow you to install your own CGI scripts, but don't provide a library. Others don't allow you to add any CGIs. I recommend that you find a company that at least allows you to add your own.

Do I Get Access Reports?

Access reports show you information about visitors to your site. You need this information, as it can show you where visitors are coming from, when they arrive, which pages they view, and so on. Some companies send reports to you automatically via e-mail each day or week. Some create charts to show access information.

Can I Have Password-Protected Pages?

If you need to set up a private area at your Web site, some companies will help you create password-protected areas. This is quite easy to do for yourself using Microsoft Frontpage.

Do You Have Telephone Technical Support?

Ask about the type of technical support available. Can you call and talk with someone? And if so, is it a toll-free or local call? This is a significant issue, as you'll almost certainly have to get help at some point. Some Web-hosting services try to handle all their support through e-mail, but the problem with this is that it's too easy to ignore e-mail or delay responses. You must have some way to talk to someone. Toll-free calls are relatively rare for low-cost Web-hosting companies; you may end up having to use a long-distance number, but that's better than nothing is. Some companies will charge you for phone support.

Chapter 2

The Internet's Free Education System

"The wind and the waves are always on the side of the navigator"

—Edward Gibbon

If you're not familiar with the Internet or you want to learn about a specific field, it's time you went back to college. Now your saying to yourself you're either too old, you don't have the time, or you just don't have the money!

Then all I have to say is that you haven't been looking in the right places. So let me steer you in the right direction. The university that I am talking about is FREE U. Actually they are better known to the Internet as discussion groups and news groups.

I have learned more in the past two years by subscribing to these discussion and news groups then I would going to a 4 year marketing college. When I think of these discussion groups the word "community" comes to my mind. That is what discussion groups are, people helping people and interacting with each other.

Discussion and news groups are places you can go to, where you can ask a specific question of about any topic you can think of and get a multitude of answers or helpful hints.

If you are new to the Internet, the discussion and news groups, you will soon see that the world isn't as big as one once thought. The Internet with its worldwide reach has opened up many doors for people, who once thought they were secluded to one area of the world.

Through these discussion and news groups I have met many new friends and business associates. I have learned of things such as merchant accounts, bulk e-mail and targeted e-mail, affiliate programs and how they work. I have learned that advertising is not just writing a few lines and then submitting it.

Three years ago I was pushed out of my comfort zone, when the company that I had worked for 18 years decided to pull up stakes and move to a city an hour away. I knew that I didn't want to lose over two hours a day commuting. My children were at the age that they were in a lot of academic and sports activities, some of which I was an active part in and by doing the commute thing I would not be able to focus on my family as I wanted to. My son taught me a few basic computer skills, showed me how to log on to the Internet and three years later I have published three books. I am now running a successful full time business over the Internet that I wouldn't give up for the world, because that is what I have at my finger tips, access to the world, thanks to the Internet and the discussion groups that I subscribe to.

I have many people to thank that have taken participation in these discussion groups and filled my brain with the knowledge of how to run a business over the Internet. But the people most responsible are the moderators that over see these discussion groups. Their hard work often goes by unnoticed, by saving us many hours a day sending us e-mail posts sometimes up to twenty daily. From these posts sent think of hundreds, maybe thousands of e-mail they receive daily. They had to sort out and decide which ones best benefited the group, so my hat goes off to them.

So how do you do know which discussion groups to sign up for and how to do it? Here are some Websites for you to visit, but don't be overwhelmed with the amount of lists available. One more thing to bring up is the fact that you can market your business or service through participation in these discussion and news groups. Now I don't mean advertise in them, I mean market your business in them. I will show you later in this chapter how to do this step by step.

Discussion Groups and Lists

First I am going to give you the Website addresses and information of my own personal favorite discussion groups. These are the discussion groups, which you will want to subscribe to if you are running a business on the Internet.

http://www.internetadvertising.org/subscribe.html

The Internet Advertising Discussion List is an E-Mail discussion on various aspects of the Internet advertising industry, including online media planning and buying, ad sales, news and trends in the industry. This list is moderated by Adam Boettieger and is more directed toward advertising a business on the Internet with a monthly or annual budget for paid advertising.

Discussion does *not* focus on "free" or "low budget" methods of promoting a site. This is a moderated list, meaning that it is *highly filtered* moderated by Adam Boettiger and that all posts submitted to the list are first reviewed by a human being for content relevance before being distributed to the entire list. Not everything submitted to the list will be distributed to its members.

http://www.audettemedia.com/i-sales/

Formed in November 1995, the goal of the Internet Sales Moderated Discussion List is to provide a forum for meaningful and helpful discussion of online sales issues by those engaged in the online sale of products and services. The list is moderated by John Audette, president of Multimedia Marketing Group, Inc. John strives to keep the signal-to-noise ratio as high as possible. The List publishes the I-Sales Digest, which is sent daily to subscribers—subscriptions are free.

http://www.entreworld.org/Discussions/Homepage.cfm?Channel=SY BDiscussion

By subscribing to the Discussion Group, you receive electronic mail from entrepreneurs, professional service providers and academicians from around the world who are facing many of the challenges you do as you launch your business! Perhaps more importantly, you can pose questions to other members on the list and share your perspectives on the topics discussed.

http://www.egroups.com/list/wsba-digest/

Website Banner Ads is a discussion group that discusses banner ad tactics Mark Welch is the moderator. Anything and everything you ever wanted to or need to know about banner ads are discussed in Marks digest. Go to his web site and subscribe now!

http://www.le-digest.com/

LinkExchange Daily Digest is a moderated discussion list focused on web site promotion and driving traffic to web sites. Digests are published five days a week. There are currently over 100,000 subscribers to the Daily Digest.

Some of the topics discussed include:
- *Analyzing click-through*
- *International marketing*
- *Domain name*
- *Analyzing traffic data*
- *Search engines*
- *Tracking site visitors*
- *Trademark and copyright*
- *Other ways of promoting your web site*

Check out these sites and decide for yourself which discussion or news groups best fits your needs.

http://nsns.com/MouseTracks/tloml.html

This by far is the best resource to finding some of the best e-mail discussion groups on the Internet. They have some of my personal favorites, but choose for yourself ones that best suite your needs.

http://www.listtool.com/

ListTool.com is a revolutionary free tool that makes the process of subscribing, unsubscribing and sending commands to 665 mailing and discussion lists (in categories such as law, art, music, computers, news, business, humor and more) easy. You no longer have to remember which command you need to send to some obscure e-mail address to subscribe or unsubscribe from a discussion / mailing list.

http://www.dejanews.com

You can find any discussion at Deja News. Deja News is a search engine for discussion groups.

http://tile.net/lists/

Tile.net has a few different options when searching for a discussion or news groups. You can search by name, by subject, description, or by host country. It is probably the easiest to use.

http://www.reference.com/

Reference.COM makes it easy to Small Businesses / Home Offices, browse, search, and participate in more than 150,000 newsgroups, mailing lists, and web forums.

http://www.liszt.com/

This by far the largest group of lists you will find and the site is very easy to use. Listz offers over 71,000 lists.

http://www.webcom.com/impulse/list.html

This is another outstanding resource of lists.

http://www.listbot.com/cgi-bin/subscriber

View List Archives: View past messages sent out to the lists you are a member of.
- *Leave Lists: Remove yourself from a ListBot mailing list.*
- *Change Password: Change the password you use to access the ListBot system.*
- *Change E-Mail: Change e-mail address where your messages are sent to.*
- *Add E-Mail: Aliases Provide additional addresses you might send mail from for discussion lists.*

http://www.webcom.com/impulse/list.html#Search

http://www.onelist.com/

Do you want start your own mail list free?

http://www.mail-list.com/ml_order.html

Discussion groups allow any subscriber to post a message, in addition to receiving each message. So if you want to have open communications with a group of people about a certain topic, a discussion group mailing list is ideal. Belonging to e-mail discussion groups is a great way to market your business on the Internet, as well as keeping up on where your industry is headed.

These e-mail discussion groups are made up of a group of people that have joined together to discuss a particular subject that was initiated by a moderator. Not all discussion groups are moderated, and I would try to avoid subscribing with those, they seem to have more advertising mixed in than discussion. If a list goes too far advertising, it becomes useless and subscribers soon drop out.

What a moderator does he initiates a subject like "places to get a merchant account," then by e-mail the group responds with suggestions or their point of view on the subject. Their response is then e-mailed back to the moderator. Then out of hundreds of posts he picks out 15 to 20 that he thinks relate best to the subject and will be most beneficial to the group. These chosen few are put to print and sent out the group.

I personally belong to about 30 discussion groups. I have a system that lets me utilize my time better and still be able still be able to read most of the posts from each discussion group. When I am online I spend most of time marketing my business which turns out to be about 4 hours a day. Looking at my computer screen 4 hours a day is plenty, so I find it easier to print out the posts from all the discussion groups and then read them as time permits. For me that is usually when my wife and I are traveling, she drives and I catch up on the discussion groups, or about an hour before I go to bed.

By printing them out I find them much easier to read or to keep for future references. When I come across a subject, (sometimes called a thread) that is of interest to me I circle it. Then first thing in the morning, before I read my e-mail, is write a response and send it back to either the group, if I think it benefits everyone, or to the person that posted it.

Another thing you can do if you are really cramped for time and can't read them right away is to create a file or folder for the messages. When I put them in folders I designate a title for each subject, much like your web browsers do for bookmarks.

Anytime you or anyone else sends a post to the moderator each person that has subscribed will receive a list of the post. How many people are in these groups? Depending on the size of a particular group it could be seen by a couple hundred people. If it is a large group like John Audette's I-Sales group, then it will be seen by tens of thousands of people around the world. Talk about some major exposure!

When you check out the Websites that I mentioned earlier, you will see that there are thousands of groups that deal with thousands of subjects. As I stated earlier these groups are a great place to market your business on the Internet, but I think they are very enjoyable to, especially when a subject you like is discussed.

One of the potential downfalls of these e-mail discussion groups is that you could receive up to 60 0r 70 separate e-mails a day. These groups can be very time consuming, they can also clutter up your mailbox. Just to delete them takes a few minutes out of your day and those minutes do add up. The discussion groups perfect for me are the moderated ones, then you don't have to worry about deleting a lot of unnecessary e-mail.

Before you subscribe, be sure to read when and how often messages is sent out. Some of the ones that a lot of other people and I consider the "good ones" usually have a daily post. There are a few that are not readable through certain e-mail programs and have to be downloaded to a file or folder on your hard drive, most of them can be read right from your mail box.

My suggestion is to subscribe to one or two that you might be interested from the lists that I talked about earlier. Give them a month or so before you decide you don't like them. Some of the first ones I subscribed to didn't really make a lot of sense the first couple of weeks I read them. I didn't understand what people were talking about, that usually happens when you are first learning. If after a couple of weeks or a month you still are not getting anything out of the discussion group, then unsubscribe.

When subscribing to discussion group it is a good idea to jot down the subscribe or unsubscribe instructions, or you could keep them on a folder on your computer. Then if you want to unsubscribe all you do is copy and paste it into your e-mail. Most of the discussion groups that I subscribe to put this information either at the beginning or the end of the e-mail.

Some of these groups offer you the option of receiving your posts in digest version, instead of receiving your posts daily you receive them once a week. I like to read mine daily because it doesn't seem like such an insurmountable of a task, but I know of people that love the digest version. So try it both ways and decide for yourself.

OK, now you're subscribed to one or two groups, what do you do now? For people that are just starting out it is good idea just to read the post before you decide to respond (this is known as lurking). By doing this you can get a feel for the group and how they discuss certain subjects. There is a technique for this, and once you seen 20 or 30 posts you will know what I am talking about. Definitely don't hang back and never say anything. If you do something wrong the moderator will let you know, no he won't be mad at you for mistakes. Moderators take on new subscribers almost daily and they take it as part of their job to correct new people. Heck even people that have posted a lot of messages have to be reminded to keep their posts in the best interests of the group.

One thing that is strictly frowned upon and won't be tolerated is a blatant advertisement. They never make it to being posted, but they do take up a moderator's busy schedule. Discussion groups are not classified ads. NO ADVERTISING!

But there is way to market your business through discussion groups.

What you need to do when you find a subject that you think might have some input, type out your thoughts and submit your post. Don't get discouraged if your post isn't printed the first time, or every time you submit a post. No ones ever are!

So how does submitting a post market your business? It comes from your expertise on a certain thread and a little thing, called a SIG file, that you put at the end of your post. For instance, maybe your are submitting a few paragraphs on how to write a successful ad if it was a discussion group that focused on Internet advertising or writing ad copy. Another, is you can post a question to something that is being discussed or was discussed. A post should never be submitted with out your SIG file. Your Signature File are those few little lines attached to every piece of email you send out or message that you post to every discussion group, or news group, Also known as a SIG file, it can be the single most effective publicity campaign you can promote. And the least expensive!

7 Tips on How to Write A Signature File

Tip # 1) No more than 4—6 Lines

Your SIG file should consist of 4-6 lines but no more. Any more than 6 lines will be considered on the verge of being commercial, and will more than likely put your post in the trash and an e-mail from the moderator reminding you that such things won't be tolerated. Some discussion groups limit their members to only four (4) lines. Make the first four lines of your Signature the most important ones, what you always want to appear. You can always delete the last two lines when posting to those discussion groups with stricter guidelines.

Signature Files are like a business card only on the Internet it is an interactive (hyper link as recipients of your messages can instantly click on the hypertext link and visit your Web Site or send you email. Signature Files are a very inexpensive way to deliver your message to the world without being blatantly commercial. A subtle message can go a very long way.

Tip # 2) Make it count.

You only have four (4) lines or possibly six (6). In either case you need to include your name or company name, the URL of your Web Site and that leaves you two lines to convey a message. Two lines is not a lot of space for your messages. Really think hard about what you want to include and make it count! You can briefly state the nature of your business, offer something to attract their visit to your Web Site, inform them of a special offer or benefit, offer something for free or make a call to action, like visit today and 3 free reports.

Tip # 3) Making more than one Signature File

You might want to make several Signature Files for different business offers, different news groups or discussion groups or perhaps one for business E-mail and another for friends and family. For business you need contact inf. but for friends you might want to send your favorite quote or a humorous story or joke.

Tip # 4) Always include your SIG File

This is FREE exposure and you should take advantage of it whenever you can. This should be when posting to news groups or discussion groups. If people like what you have to say than they will click to your Web Site to find out more. We have had a lot of business and initial contacts that came to us straight from our SIG File, so use it wisely and as often as you can.

Tip # 5) Keep your SIG File Current

Make sure that the information in your Signature File is current! There is some email software programs that do not actually show you the SIG File being attached before you send it out. We once sent out information on a Web Site that was no longer in existence because of this characteristic in our e-mail software

Tip # 6) Code Your SIG File

It is very important to "CODE" your SIG File so that you know which of your marketing efforts is providing you with the best results. For example, let us say you visited the discussion groups and made several postings. The first group you visited you may wish to add the CODE "Item #123" and for the next one "Item #234". Make it simple so that your prospects will take the time to use it.

When other people read your article (keep it short 2 or 3 paragraphs) or your question, some may have questions or answers that pertain only to you so that is why you need a SIG file at the end of your post. Enough about where you need a SIG file, now it's time to show how to make your own SIG file and what should all be included in the SIG file.

Sample Signature File

John Doe Ad Copy by John Doe
Author How to write ad copy that will have
People begging for your products.
Newsletter http://www.adcopy.com
Free Report johndoe@adcopy.com
Phone: 111-222-3333 Fax: 333-222-1111

Attach your SIG file to the end of your post and for that matter to all your e-mail. If anyone wants to contact you about items that you have posted they now have your contact information and your SIG file tells people a little bit about your business.

John Doe could also subscribe to discussion groups that he may be interested in, but may have no connection with his products or services. For example, maybe he is interested in snow skiing. His post to this list would have to pertain to snow skiing, but he would still use the same SIG file he used for the discussion group about ad copy.

If you have 10 or 20 different free reports that you would like for people to read via e-mail for marketing purposes you could have different SIG files for each one. This is where software like Eudora Pro *http://www.eudora.com/* comes in handy. With Eudora you can setup multiple different SIG files and with the click of your mouse you can paste in whatever SIG file you want. This method of marketing can be a great source of prequalified leads and loads of fun, so enjoy.

Sometimes when you unsubscribe you will keep getting posts from the group. Sometimes even after numerous e-mails to unsubscribe have gone seemingly unnoticed some out side source can be helpful. That is when you want to contact:

http://www.cancel-it.com/

Want to cancel an e-mail discussion group Cancel-it ® is the Internet's first on-line consumer advocacy cancellation service. Use our universal form to cancel any on-line product or service – completely free of charge. Why waste hours on the phone waiting to cancel a service?

Chapter 3

Selling Your Products or Services Online

"I think the one lesson that I have learned is that there is no substitute for paying attention."

—Diane Sawyer

No matter what your product or service is, it must produce a benefit for your customers. Benefits such as saving time, saving money, helping your customers live a healthier life, or making their business ventures more profitable.

Products or Services Features and Benefits

Products and Services may be described in terms of their features and benefits. Features are products or services characteristics that deliver benefits. Features are product characteristics such size, color, profitability, functionality, design, hours of business, editorial content, etc.

Benefits answer the customers or prospects question: What's in it for me? To identify your product's benefits, you must consider the customer's viewpoint.

The 4 Objectives to Selling Your Products or Services
The Product or Service

Research is absolutely necessary when selling a product or service. Look at your product or service and list the benefits your customers will be able to attain by purchasing from you. Trade places with your customers and look at it as though you were the customer. *What type of people will purchase your products or services? Is it a small or large market?* When developing a product I try to reach a market that is of a large variety. Unless it is clear that your target market has a chance for growth, much like the Internet (the Internet started out small and continues to grow).

The Headline or Ad

Have you made an irresistible offer? Did your headline reach out and grab your prospects? Was your ad simple to read? (Leave out the fifty-dollar words). If your prospects don't understand what you are trying to say to them then the ad is worthless.

The Means

How will you get your ad out to the masses? Will you use Classifieds, Radio, Television, E-Zines, or Direct Mail? Spending a large amount of money on these forms of media will be of no use to you if don't have a good product or service. Neither will your product sell if you don't have a compelling ad.

The Customer

What type of people is your product or service best suited for? Will hockey players be interested in baby pacifiers? I don't think so. Research who your target markets is.

What is a USP?

USP stands for Unique Selling Proposition. Your USP is the exact benefit your customers get when they purchase one of your products or services. Your USP is what separates what you are selling apart from the exact same products or services that your competitors sell. Here are a few examples of USP statements:

- **Fireman:** "Fire extinguishers designed and built by a retired fireman"
- **Dietitian:** "Foods that you should avoid".
- **Professional Carpet Cleaner:** "How to remove odors from your carpet"

Remember that your USP is a respected advertising philosophy, standing for Unique Selling Proposition. In short, it is the one definition that you give your customers to buy from you instead of from your competitors. You can work it out by formulating a sentence that begins: "Buy from me because my company is the ONLY one that (includes your USP here). In Internet marketing, a USP is critical. For most products and services, Internet customers can buy just as easily from a company in England as they can from you.

Your Shipment

O.K. now you have sold your products, the next step is the shipment. There are fulfillment houses that can handle this for you. By using a fulfillment house you can save yourself time, but when using a fulfillment house they leave out an important segment. A thing that you can do that a fulfillment house can't is adding that personal touch. What I like to do when shipping a product is to put my company name and logo on each and every package that I send out. I also include my contact information in the package, Website address, E-mail address, Phone number and return address if there was a problem in shipping the product that may be returned. The last and probably the most important thing are I send a hand written thank you note. I have received many compliments by using this personal touch. Your customers really appreciate knowing that they are more than just another sale.

If you decide that you would rather have a fulfillment house ship your products I suggest you visit Fulfillment Services Website at:

http://www.fill-it.com/

Here is a list of items that they specialize in:

- Literature Fulfillment
- Merchandise Fulfillment
- E-Commerce
- Quality Control
- Lead and Inquiry Response
- Trade Show Fulfillment
- Technical Reference Service
- Technology Overview

- Implementation Programs
- Custom Reporting
- Computer Services and Software
- Consulting Services
- Association Fulfillment

Fulfillment is particularly one of the least discussed aspects of Internet commerce, in spite of the fact that consumer surveys rank speed of delivery as one of their top priorities when purchasing goods and services online. Many companies seem to neglect this phase especially home based business that are just starting out.

Global Shipping

If you are selling products or services on the World Wide Web be prepared to ship your products or services globally. Most never give this a thought until they receive an order from another country. Here are a couple of companies that can assist you in meeting your international shipping orders:

Global Shipping & Freight International
http://www.gsfi.qpg.com/

Receive 10% off if you mention you found them on the Internet.

Federal Express
http://www.fedex.com/us/services/

One of the old reliable companies.

http://www.aloha.com/~business/global.htm

They offer USA to World Wide Air Freight and Ocean Freight Service

United Parcel Service
http://www.ups.com/using/services/intl/intl-guide.html

http://www.aajs.com/shipnet/

Chapter 4

How To Build A Monster Moneymaking Web Site that WILL keep you're Customers Coming Back For More

"Look at the word blame. It's just coincidence that the last two letters
spell the word me. But that coincidence is worth thinking about.
Other people or unfortunate circumstances may have caused you to feel pain,
but only you control whether you allow that pain to go on.
If you want those feelings to go away, you have to say: "Its up to me"

—Dr. Arthur Freeman and Rose DeWolf

The first things to decide is whether to build the site yourself or have a Web Designer do it for you. This all depends on your level of computer skills and understanding of computer software. There are some tremendous advantages to building your own site. Not only is it cheaper but you gaining valuable knowledge on how a web site is built. Then you can build Web pages or Websites for people for **MONEY.**

Building Your Own Website

So you have thought it over and decided your going to take the plunge and build your own Website. You can surf the web and look at a ton of sites to see what type of Website you think is displayed well. But your asking what is it I should look for? It is better to look at some examples, using URL (Universal Resource Locator) type this web address in. *http://www.webpagesthatsuck.com* These are Websites that you definitely don't want your site to look at.

Should I Get My Own Domain Name?

This will give your business its own identity. Internic's new domain registration of $70.00 for 2 years, which is $35.00 per year or $2.92 per month (you will have to pay for your first two years in advance) is one of the best investments you'll make. Especially, if you are planning to sell a product or service online and you are not spending the $2.92 per month for your own domain, what are you spending it on?

The second reason for having your own domain is that if you ever have to change hosting services for whatever reason your printed material will not have to be reprinted. Just transferred from one ISP to another. You won't lose all the effort you have taken into publicizing your e-mail and Website on stationary, envelopes and through many other publications. In addition the people that you don't even remember that have visited your site over the years and have it book marked will still be able to contact your Website. These are all things that you could stand to lose along with some major income, by not having your own domain name.

If the $70.00 is too much for your budget and for some people, like myself, when first starting out it can be expensive. You can do something a little bit different and still have your domain name to fit your business.

At TJ Network (*http://www.tjns.tj*) for example, you can use a domain name with any type of Website, free or otherwise, using the redirection service also called Site DNS. This costs just $8.00 a year if using a com/net/org domain name. They will give you a name under their com.tj or web.tj sub domains. There is no setup fee so the annual $8.00 is your only fee. And for $8.00 a year more they will redirect e-mail sent to your domain to whatever e-mail address you specify. This may not be the most popular thing to do but, the main thing is to get your site up and running for as little as possible if your marketing budget is tight.

Other redirection services that are reputable are:

http://www.ontheweb.nu/
http://www.come.to/
http://home.ml.org

In looking at the Big Picture, for both my business and myself, there was never a question about where to spend my money. Just a word to the wise, if the hosting company or a private individual is registering for your domain name make darn sure that you are the administrator of that domain name.

There have been some companies and individuals that have registered other people's domain names and named themselves as the administrator. These people are in total control of your Website and if they wish to they can have your Website totally deleted from your Internet Service Provider. If anyone charges you more than the $70.00 per domain they are padding their own pocket.

How Hard Is It To Build My Own Website?

With the new computer software packages for Web Design such as Microsoft Frontpage 98, which is my favorite, it is so user friendly. All of the hard things one would used to need to know like HTML Frontpage automatically takes care of it for you. If you are worried about needing to know HTML (Hypertext Markup Language) or how to pick a background or what type or size of font to use worry no farther. Most webpage authoring programs come with a set of templates you can use—simply open, add your text, and save it as a new file.

Frontpage has great tutorials that guides you along every step of the way until your new Web Site or pages are completed, looking like a professionally finished product. Check out Microsoft's Web Site and you can get a demo download for free, so try it out. Go to the web site at *http://www.Microsoft.com/frontpage*

For more information on building your site. A good place to go on AOL is HTML and Web Publishing Tools. **Keyword: HTML**

For more Free things to download to help you build your Websites check out this site: *http://www.hotfiles.com/hot/free100.html* and download these Free pieces of software Arachnophilia and Webthing

Another software program is *Adobe Page Mill 3.0* check out their Website *http://www.adobe.com/prodindex/pagemill/regwina.html* most Internet Service Providers offer their version of web page design, check with them to be sure. They may not offer what Frontpage and Adobe Paper Mill offer but if your just starting out with a very small budget, it can be worth checking them out.

Free WebPages and Websites

If you are just starting out and you are running on a tight budget here is a list of places to obtain free places to build you Webpage or Website.

http://www.angelfire.com/

This site contains a lot of free things for your Website. Be sure to read the FAQ this will be a big help in answering any questions you may have.

http://www.tripod.com/

By joining Tripod you will receive 2MB of web space. You can use their editor, or write your own HTML. They also have Chat Rooms. Just one thing to remember, when someone goes to a members page, they will automatically see a Tripod advertisement. However, it is a free web space.

http://www.geocities.com/join/

Get an address in one of their Cities or suburbs for free. Address includes a 2MB Home site and FREE e-mail. Type in this URL and find out more why Geocities is probably one of the best free sites you will find on the Web. *http://www.geocities.com/main/help/geotour/*

http://www.webspawner.com/

You can get a FREE Webpage. That's right, only one page per address for now, but they are in the process of expanding to give you more than just one page. On the upside, you can have multiple addresses. Only 25k text spaces per page so keep it simple.

http://www.upws.com/

A new Australian based site and the last time I checked their Free Sites were full but they are going to add more.

http://www.freeyellow.com/faq/start.html

Free Yellow ranks right up there with Geocities as far what they offer. You can get a ton of free things with your Free Yellow site.

Free auto-responders (I'll tell you how to use these in a later chapter), Free Graphics, Free Counters, and Free E-mail order forms.

http://www.spree.com/

A fast growing free Web spaces provider that also offers MLM-type moneymaking opportunities (I will be checking this out at a later date to see if it is legitimate). Note: click on the "Your Free Website" link to get your free page. Although Spree claims to offer "unlimited space," they do, in fact, have a two-megabyte limit. Spree offers other freebies, such as a guest book, a counter and a directory manager.

Spree is also offering a popular partners program, in which you can earn commissions for sending traffic their way. (Check out my Affiliates listings in an upcoming chapter).

Your Home Page

Personally I find it very annoying to go to a Website and first thing to see are some large graphics and image to click on just to get to the content of the site. This may not be a problem in a few years when we go to fiber optics and things will download at the speed of light or even faster than a 14.4 Modem, until then keep the first page for content and customer benefits.

Things You Must Have On Your Website to Make Money

1) Close to the bottom of your home page you need to have a place to capture your visitors e-mail address. After they fill out the form for their e-mail address have a button next to the box that will send them to your second page. With this method you get the critical information on page one then you try for more questions on page two. If people drop out on page two or three that's OK, because you have already obtained the most critical information, their e-mail address.

2) A call to action by this I mean a stirring statement that will move your visitors into making a purchase.

3) Have more than just one item to purchase. What if all I have is one item to purchase? I will discuss later several affiliate companies that will pay you for selling their products.

4) Selling advertising on your site is another way of creating income for you and it costs nothing. One or two banner ads on your pages are plenty so don't over do it. Remember you worked hard to get your visitors to your site don't lose them to a ton of banner ads.

5) Create a form on your home page that asks what your prospects want, why they want it, and how much they are willing to pay? Use that information to your advantage. What better way to grow your business than to give people what they want and what better way to find out what people want than to ask them?

Basically you are finding where and who your market is and presenting them with the benefits of your service or product. Again, being online gives you that vehicle to grow your business to heights you have never dreamt of.

6) Always ask your visitors to bookmark your Website. Let them know that your site will always be updated on a regular basis, to offer new content and products and be sure to follow through with what you promise them. Never offer more than what you can deliver. This will give you major credibility and you will gain new prospects by word of mouth.

7) Give them your company name, street address, or post office box, phone number, fax number, and e-mail address.

8) Get an 800 number for your orders, and the use of an answering machine if your budget is tight. However, if they can talk to someone live or have an operator with a fulfillment house it is an advantage and it will make your business have that real professional look. An 800 number will help increase the confidence of your prospective buyers and it can increase your sales by at least 200%.

I personally use **Matrix Telecom PO Box 880100 Dallas, Texas 75388-0100; 1-800-282-0242**. I find their service and support to be nothing less than professional and rates are 9.9 cents per minute.

A word of caution you don't want to get into changing long distance companies every two or three months. Find a good one and stick with them. Remember your customers are your primary concern.

9) Accepting a credit card is a must (a minimum of two is required examples would be MasterCard and Visa). This can boost your sales by as much as 300%. The process does not have to be automated until you start getting a large number of orders.

10) Offer a guarantee with your products or service. The longer the guarantee the more sales it will produce. I offer a 1 year 100% money back guarantee. I'm confident that what I teach works and it takes time to use everything that I offer. If you offer a 30-day guarantee your customers will hurry through the service and may not be able to give it the time it takes to work for them.

11) When writing content for your site use short paragraphs to keep the readers interest. Using margins will increase readership even though it increases the price of your print. We really don't have to worry about that on the Internet unless you have someone else build your site. In the long run it can increase your sales by making your content easier to read.

12) Never use caps in an entire sentence, on the Internet that is considered screaming. If you use caps in a single word, use it only to emphasize a word.

22 Things That Should Never Appear On A Business Website

#1 Items of no value

Never sell items that are of no benefit to your targeted market i.e. if you are selling informational items, would you want to offer vitamins or unrelated items of this nature? Give your customers a good reason to buy from you.

#2 Large Graphics On Your Home Page

You have either spent a lot of time or money or both on creating your Website. Give your customers a chance to at least get into your home page that is why you built it in the first place so they could get into it and see what you have so you can do business with them. Remember your future customers may come from all walks of life. Some may be high tech wizards with supersonic computers, with lightening fast modems. Others will have used equipment with maybe the modem placed on sale from two years ago.

Large graphics take longer to load up, if it takes too long load, do you think that they will wait for this web site to load up. Most people are impatient and if a Website takes longer than 30 seconds at the very most to load up they will click off of it and go on to another site.

Here are the average load times for the various modems.

- **1.4K** 433.8 seconds
- **28.8K** 18.6 seconds
- **56.6K** 12.7 seconds
- **ISDN** 128K 4.5 seconds
- **T1** 1.4 seconds

Check with *Website Garage* at the bottom of this page to see where your site stacks up. Remember have it load at 30 seconds or less to keep those prospects.

#3 Free Reports Or Free Product Orders Not Sent Out Immediately

If you want to be successful consider offering your customers something free. Think of the free product or service as a trial package to see if they like or want what you're trying to sell them. Not only will you get a customer database built up fast but you'll keep them coming back. If however you fail to deliver immediately, you not only lose you credibility with them and future sales but word of mouth can be great or extremely deadly.

#4 Sites That Receive Awards for Being the Best

People aren't interested in what you have done. They are interested in what you can do for them. Sell them on the benefits of the products you have. A happy customer is one that will keep coming back.

#5 Website Under Construction

This is a big **NO NO! Never** advertise your Website until it is completely done. Websites that are incomplete are big turnoffs for anyone. Do this and your customers and potential customers, along with your creditability, are history. You should give your customers to a call to action once your website is complete.

#6 Company Logos Or Welcome To My Site

Way to many sites have company logos plastered all over their home page or "Welcome to my site banners" this a waste of space, but your customers don't give a hoot about a colorful logo. They are interested about what you have that will benefit them. Keep these annoying things off of your home page.

#7 Marquees, Spinning Balls, Counters, etc.

These are great things that computer design professionals say your web site needs, however they do nothing for selling your products. Marquees and Spinning balls do the same thing for your site. Absolutely nothing, except take up space and take forever for your page to load up.

Those really nifty counters, another space waster. No one cares how many times your page has been visited except for you. That is something you can ask your ISP. They offer stats that will tell you where your customers are coming from, what pages they have visited, and how long they have stayed at each page. This will help you in keeping your Website up to date with information that people are looking for. It will also help you decide what pages or content to delete.

#8 Don't Use These Words or Words like Them

"Again your company name, my, we, us, I, our, us" Do you understand why? These are words pertain to you and not your customers. Remember your customers only care about their benefits, not you or anyone else. This may not always be possible, but here is a ratio you should use if you have to use these words. For every one of them use words like you 3-4 times more.

#9 Your Name, Address And Phone Number At The Top Of Any Page

Use these for specific purposes only, such as to call for consulting or any additional information. It's best to put it at the bottom of the page, after an article or report, or if they have to call for product purchases. For no other reason should any of this information be listed. Customers don't care where you are from unless it has a benefit for their needs.

#10 Grammar Or Typographical Errors

Your Website, reports, articles, should be reviewed closely. Errors are a reflection on you. Your striving to be perceived as someone who knows what you are doing and your commitment to excellence. When I develop a Website for someone or when I type reports or articles I use Microsoft Word, it thankfully has a spelling checker, it has saved me from looking like an uneducated fool many times.

#11 Frames

Frames are another Website gadget that makes loading up very slow. Some of the old browsers don't support frames any longer, making your Website unreadable. Some search engines don't support frames either. If you find a need to use frames, I'll have a special report on what search engines support frames and which ones don't. Most frames require scrolling bars that can take up valuable space.

#12 External Links To Other Websites

"Not on my home page" After you have placed a ton of ads trying to get people to your Website the last thing you want to do is place an external link to someone else's Website. Once you get people to your Website keep them there so they will look and hopefully buy from you. You built your site to sell to others, not to send them elsewhere. There will be times when you want to link to other sites for your customers benefit (I really like that word) but place these links on later pages.

#13 Broken Links

These rank right up there with typographical errors. There's no need for them. So double-check your site for broken links. Here is an example of a good link and a broken one: http://www.yourpage.com now the bad one http://www.your page.com

#14 Missing Or Incomplete Graphics

If you must use graphics use smaller ones that load up fast and make sure there is nothing missing. This is almost like leaving a chapter out of a book, it leaves a potential customer wondering what was suppose to be there.

#15 Extra Long Home page

If a home page goes on forever it will send your customers fleeing. Wondering when the next page will finally come up. Keep it about 3K in size, this seems to be just about right. If you do use frames your customers won't be scrolling down forever. Something I like to do at the bottom of every page is to offer the customers 3 or 4 different ways to pay for the products I sell. If your pages are too long, then you may just lose some sales and you don't want one customer to leave before they have had a chance to buy at least 1 item.

#16 Java Script

This is another one of those things that seems to take forever to load up. Think of those with the older computers and the slow modems. Well here's another thing to consider, you've heard of Web TV? It's here and growing fast as ever and web surfers who have this will think there is something wrong with your home page. Sorry but Web TV, for now, does not support Java Script or Pop Up Windows, and it won't until after the year 2000. So "no javascript for now."

#17 Confusing or Non-Secure Order Forms

It's best not to accept credit cards if you don't have secure forms. If you sell more than 3 or 4 items set your site up with a shopping cart system. Its easier for ordering and the best way to sell is to make it as simple as possible.

#18 Plagiarized Reports, Articles, Or Books

Just to keep your nose clean and be everything a customer wants you to be above all is Honest. Too many people take copyrighted material and copy it as their own. Not only is it dishonest but you can legally get in trouble by doing this. I want you to stay in business forever because it's just as important to me to have you as a return customer and not one who has to waste his/hers hard earned money on attorneys fees and not on my future products. Besides most people will flattered to let you put their materials on your site as long as they can have there name and e-mail address on the bottom of it.

#19 Lengthy and Complex URL's

Surveys and studies have been taken and their conclusions are that people prejudge a site by the URL. So keep the when deciding on a URL make sure it compliments what your site is all about and the shorter the URL the easier it will be for people to remember.

#20 Provide a Site Map

All too often Websites are created without a clear picture of how all the components are supposed to fit together. A lack of clear organization of a Website will only confuse and frustrate people to the point that they will leave your sight never to return. Remember that if you are going to use an image map as a navigational tool, have some text links (these should be blue, don't deviate form what is common practice throughout the WWW) somewhere on the page. The reason for this is that search engines cannot follow the links inside an image map. You may be wondering why does this make a difference? Some search engines determine how high your site is ranked based on your links. So check out what things each search engine requires.

#21 Website with Old Information

Change your content frequently and offer your customers new reasons to return to your site. Remember the Internet changes almost daily. Believe me it will be well worth the time spent when your customers keep coming back and bring their friends with them. The doors of opportunity will be swinging wide open.

#22 Patterned Backgrounds

Personal preference with Websites is understandable. However, you need to recall that the site is to be more for your customers. Online marketers stay with a white background since this resembles newspaper editing and we are competing with newspapers in a sense.

White backgrounds are much easier on the readers eyes and we want to keep people at our sites as long as possible. Remember " Content is King " on any marketing Website. With that in mind lets remember that in order to make a sale from your Website it is important that your home page catches the customers eye in 30 seconds or less. Yes, 30 seconds or less if you don't have some great content and most of all some great benefits for your customers; they will click on to some other web page.

Include the 3 C's

- **Community**

These are the types of people that your Website attracts. These visitors want the items or services that your Website offers. By offering features and benefits, maybe a newsletter, or some free report. It is by search engine placement with the proper key-words used when submitting your Website, or from a classified that will attract a certain segment of people that will build your online community.

- **Content**

This should be well planned out, well written and frequently updated with new products, and new articles to keep your old customers coming back as well as keeping up or ahead of Websites with similar items or services.

- **Context**

This refers to what it is your offering and how it pertains to your target market. The rule of thumb, don't sell kitchen utensils if you are an automotive store. Whatever it is that your selling, you should list 5 of your best products or services and list the benefits these products can do for your customers. I suggest using bullets this keeps your products separated. It is easy to distinguish from the others, because you won't sell all of your products to everyone even if though that should be your goal.

HERE'S THE WAY I USE BULLETS

- How You Can Lose 100 lbs. In 3 Weeks: Click **here** to get a free report on how super duper weight control will help you achieve this.
- **Discover how you can cut 30 minutes off your Yard mowing:** Get your free report on how the Handy Dandy Blade will cut your mowing time in half. Click here **Now!**

By giving your prospects a call to action and something free it is almost impossible for anyone not to read on any farther. You've gotten their attention and now they want to stay at your site to find out what this is all about.

An idea for more good things to give away on your home page is a weekly or biweekly or monthly newsletter. Not only will they respond to another free article but also in your newsletter you can speak of other new products that will help them make their **Online business boom.**

Newsletters are really easy to put together and they will keep you in touch with your newly found Prospect. The best thing about a newsletter is that you are gaining credibility with your customers. There are free articles all over the Internet that you can use in your newsletter.

One other item you should have for your customers is a comment box for your clients' opinions. This is very important because you need to know what your customers want for products or services. Asking them what they would like to see adds to your site, making your customers feel that you set them above money making. That is one of my most valuable assets, my customers input and it should be right at the top of your list to.

Back to the home page. After you set up your content and your navigational tools to tour your home page and other pages of you Website you need to include some of the last and some of the most important things to have on your home page.

How are your customers going to pay for the products? This should be on every page of your web site. You want to make things as easy as possible for them to buy from you. Offer payment to you in these forms:

- **Credit Cards**
- **Checks by Fax, Phone, or E-mail**
- **Money Orders**
- **Phone in Orders**

Phone in Orders by use of a fulfillment house. Here is a couple that I highly recommend:

Fulfillment Services
1955 West Grand Road
Tucson, Arizona 85745
520-798-1513

Fill It, Inc.
Chicago, Illinois
630-406-5900
http://www.fill-it.com

Fill-it offers the widest variety of services

Don't forget to put up an order form with all your products. You can either have this on your home page or as a link to another page with your catalog or products list. All of these payment options along with a business number or 800# must be offered 24 hours a day and seven days a week. The reason, not all people conduct their business during the day. Some people work 2nd and 3rd shifts at their regular job and may be doing something else in their leisure time.

The last thing to make sure you have on your home page and every other page of your site is a way to get back to the home page, your contact information: The name of your business. Your name, your off-line or physical address, phone number. Your e-mail address and of course, your Website address.

Congratulations! You have just completed your Website and now it is time to upload it to your Internet Service provider right? Wrong, you need to have everything checked over. Spelling, content to make sure it is grammatically correct. Are you saying to your self not another expensive bill? Well there is are two excellent Websites to do this for you and it won't cost you an arm and a leg. *http://www.websitegarage.com/* and *http://www.submitplus.com/sitetest.htm*

Go to the tune up pages of The Website Garage and Submit Plus and have these items checked out.

Critical Diagnostic Checks:
Tune Up runs the following on up to 20 pages of your site
Browser Compatibility
Verify that your Web site will display
in different browsers and versions.
!Register-It! Readiness
Make sure your site is ready to be indexed and submitted
to the top search engines and directories.
Load Time Check—reports load time from 14.4K to T1.
Dead Link Check—detect hard to find dead links.
Link Popularity Check—find out how many
sites are linking to you.
Spell Check—catch misspelled words.
HTML Check—how does your design compare to the best

Here are a couple of other sites that do the same or similar checks that offer a **FREE** service.

http://www.gumball-tracker.com/?uk
http://www.netmechanic.com
http://www.cast.org/bobby/
http://www.keynote.com/wp1.html

Building a Web Site seems to be over my head

Do you have neither the time or desire to build a Web Site? Do you think its just something you can't do? You can give me a call at **1-402-423-7607** or e-mail me at *bbrolhorst@wave5marketing.com*

I'll be more than happy to build you a moneymaking Website or refer you to some of my star Webmaster designers.

Wave 5 Marketing
c/o Bob Brolhorst
5449 Sugarberry Court
Lincoln, Nebraska 68516
1-888-445-9291
bbrolhorst@wave5marketing.com

Chapter 5

How to Write Knockout Headlines That Prospects Can't Turn Away From

"How do you go from where you are to where you want to be?
I think you have to have an enthusiasm for life.
You have to have a dream, a goal, and you have to be willing to work for it."

—Jim Valvano

How do you write a headline that will attract new customers into replying to read your sales letter? This probably the most important part of your marketing campaigns, without getting people to read further then the rest doesn't really matter. Listen carefully and by the end of this chapter I will have you writing headlines that will have people reading your ad.

It all depends on how to word your headline. There are words that people respond to better than others and is what you will want to start your headline with.

USE STRONG HEADLINES

Your headline is everything whether you are writing an ad, sales letter, or even an article to be published. The key to success is your headlines. You must understand that the wording of your headline is more than 90% of the effectiveness of your advertising. That means it is a **VERY BIG DEAL what** your headline says.

Here is something else to take into consideration. In direct marketing, it has been my experience that negative headlines often out pull positive headlines. For example, one of the most popular and effective headlines in network marketing has been "Dead Down lines Don t Lie!" If you are selling health and nutrition products This headline would be a good one "If You Are Over Weight and Stuck In a Rut." But there are situations when you want to use a positive headline. For example "Discover How You Can Double Your Income in 6 Months" or "How to advertise for FREE Online".

Negative headlines force your prospect to identify with them saying, " Hey that sounds like me. Don't forget the positive ones when used right can be just as powerful. The main purpose of the headline is to **GRAB** their attention, so your headline must be attention grabbing and prospect focused.

What are your customers needs? What are their desires? What are their Fears? Pay attention. Learn what your customers want. Headlines will make or break your online and off-line business career! But to know what works the best you have to **TEST! TEST! TEST!**

How can you test your headlines? Once you are satisfied with your top three headlines test them by preparing three separate ads changing only the headline. If you don't do this you will never realize the potential of your marketing dollars and whether one headline is better than the other is. Even if you have a found a headline that pulls in more prospects, you should continue to work on your headlines. You will never get everyone to read your ad. By changing your headline at different intervals you may hit other people hot buttons that you didn't reach before. It is a part of your marketing scheme that never ends.

So what is it that makes a compelling headline? It has everything to do with the words you use and how you use them. Certain words like **FREE, Discover, Discount,** or phrases such as: For a limited time, Limited Offer, If you read this or how you can. Remember your most powerful benefit should be incorporated into your headline.

100 MAGICAL WORDS THAT SELL!!!

Add sale punch to describe your merchandise or sales offer by using one of the following words. It may be helpful, used alone, or with other words. They have been selected from a combination of successful advertisements, books and magazines for your use in preparing some great headlines that draw people to your ad or sales letter.

Absolutely. Amazing. Approved. Attractive. Authentic. Bargain. Beautiful. Better.Big.Colorful.Colossal.Complete.Confidential.Crammed.Delivered Direct. Discount. Easily. Endorsed. Enormous. Excellent. Exciting. Exclusive. Expert.. Famous. Fascinating. Fortune. Full. Genuine. Gift. Gigantic. Greatest. Guaranteed. Helpful. Highest. Huge. Immediately. Improved. Informative. Instructive. Interesting. Largest. Latest. Lavishly. Liberal. Lifetime. Limited. Lowest. Magic. Mammoth. Miracle. Noted. Odd. Outstanding. Personalized. Popular. Powerful. Practical. Professional. Profitable. Profusely. Proven. Quality. Quickly. Rare.

Reduced. Refundable. Remarkable. Reliable.. Revealing.
Revolutionary. Scarce.. Secrets.. Security..
Selected..Sensational.. Simplified..
Sizable..Special..Startling..Strange..Strong..Sturdy...Successful..Supe
rior..Surprise.Terrific..Tested..Tremendous..Unconditional..Unique..U
nlimited.. Unparalleled.. Unsurpassed.. Unusual.. Useful..Valuable..
Wealth.. Weird.. Wonderful.

THE 89 MOST THREATENING WORDS

Recommend.. occurred.. principal.. equipped..accommodate..
disappoint.. possession.. privilege..inconvenience.. accept..
business.. necessary.. personal..
receive.. reference.. separate.. their.. whether.. criticism.. description..
effect.. extension..judgment.. quantity.. similar.. undoubtedly.. height.
immediately. stationery.. foreign.. government. omitted. personnel..
existence.. analysis..
across.. appearance.. loose.. practical. preferred. unnecessary.. affect..
attendance.. incidentally. apparent. calendar.. strictly.. principle.
already. coming.. its. oblige. opportunity.. original. paid. probably..
referred.. there.. too..
writing.. among.. arrangement.. practically.. convenient. canceled.
using.. beginning.. especially. volume. committee. confident..
difference.. endeavor..
explanation.. except.. sincerely.. experience.. benefited. conscientious.
eligible.. acquaintance.. controversy. exceed. laboratory.. omission..
procedure.. Acknowledgment. Guarantee. schedule.

The Second Most Important Item in Advertising

The ad itself is the 2nd most important item. In fact the ad is just an extension of your headline. The best way to write a powerful compelling ad is to list 5 of your best benefits for your products or service.

If you want an ad that works, do this:

FOLLOW THE AIDA RULE

This formula has withstood the test of time, and should always be followed if the purpose of the ad is to create a response on the part of the reader.

AIDA stands for, in order:
1. Getting Attention from your readers for your products or services.
2. Creating Interest in your readers for your products or services.
3. Creating a Desire on the part of your reader for your products or services.
4. Getting an Action from the reader to start on the steps in obtaining your products and services.

Your ad is of no use if one of the above components is missing in your ad, or they are not in the order as mentioned above.

Five Rules when writing Your Ad

Rule # 1

All of your ads must make a demanding proposition to the potential customer. Not with empty words that offer no benefit, but with honest and truthful intentions. Your readers should get this impression, but this product and you will get this specific benefit.

Rule # 2

The proposition has to be one that your competition does not offer, this is known as the USP (Unique Selling Proposition).

Rule # 3

The proposition must be so strong that it can attract new customers to your product or service.

Rule # 4

Write your ad just as if you were speaking to and attempting to sell just one person. Don't let your ad sound as a public speaker addressing a huge assembly filled with people, but as if there were just one individual "listening."Don't try to be overly clever, brilliant or humorous in your advertising. Keep your copy simple, to the point, and on target.

Rule # 5

The last order of business is to study your competition, take a look how they are selling their products or services. Practice rewriting their ads from a different point of view or from a different sales angle. Keep a file of ads you've clipped from different publications in a file of ad writing ideas. But don't copy anyone else's work; just use the ad material of others to stimulate your own creativeness.

60 CALL TO ACTION PHRASES

End your ad with a call to action phrase. Give the inquirer a number to call or an e-mail address to respond to or a button to push here is 60 definite ways to get action. Don't read them just once read them 3 or four times so they are embedded in your subconscious.

Act now! Send your name. Free for you. Amazing products. Free. Ask for free report. Informative lists sent free. Free book. Free catalog. Details completely free. Current listings free. Dealers e-mail for prices. Description sent free. Details free! Dime brings free description. Products supplied! Exciting details free. First lesson, 5 cents. Information folders free! For free literature write. Free booklet tells all. Free plans show you how. Free wholesale plan. Free with approvals. Get facts that help. . Get yours wholesale. Gifts with purchases. Get your free copy now. Interesting details free. Investigate today. Its Free! Act Now! Mail requests now: Money making information free. No obligation! Write! Limited offer! Send today. Only 5 cents to introduce. Order direct from: Order Now! Don't Delay! Request free literature. Revealing booklet free. Sales kit furnished. Sample details free. Samples sent on trial. See before you buy. Send for free details. Send for it today. Send no money. Send 32 cents for mailing. Send today. Send your wish lists. My Stamp brings details. Stamped envelope brings. Try tested lesson free. Unique free offers. Valuable articles free. Write for booklet free. Write us first! Yours for the taking just ask. 32 cent stamps for details.

The Key is to combine your words: EXAMPLE: "THE DAILY DIRECT DELIVER"; "The Three "D" Program"...This has already caught the attention and interest of your prospect! Now, for example say' "The Money Saving Facts are FREE! Merely enclose your check or money order!" Fill in with a few details and you have a tremendous Money Pulling Ad. Use your own Ideas, but build them around these words and word phrases! But remember, your follow-up material, must be just as interesting to get the to keep your customers interest.

One last thing to remember: The summer months when people are most likely to be away on vacation are usually not good months for Internet or direct mail. But they ARE good for opportunity and advertisements in publications often found in vacation areas, and in motels and hotels.

I can't stress this too much or too often: Success in any business online or off-line does indeed depend upon advertising, and as with anything else, quality pays off in the long run. Read this chapter again; study it; let it sink in. Then apply the principles outlined in it. They have worked for others, and **THEY CAN WORK FOR YOU!**

Chapter 6

Setting Up an E-mail Account with an Autoresponders

"Neither you nor the world knows what you can do until you have tried."

—Ralph Waldo Emerson

Now that we have set up your Website, we need to set up an e-mail account. If you are online with **America Online, CompuServe,** or **Prodigy,** these servers are great for information sources. Or to just generally have fun, but they will shut your account down if you send or receive more than 1000 e-mails a day. If you use this home study course as I have outlined it you will be sending and receiving more than that. If you plan on doing bulk e mailing here are some places where you can sign up for free e-mail? Some of them have free Autoresponders, something you will need that I will explain later in this chapter.

Places To Get Free E-mail Accounts

Bigfoot: *http://www.bigfoot.com*

You *can have multiple address names and all of the mail sent to one central account and it does not even have to be a Bigfoot account.*

Net Address: *http://www.usa.net*

Vlaise: *http://www.valise.com*

Hotmail: *http://www.hotmail.com*

Hotmail offers more for their services. This is a very popular company based on the fact that they sign up sixty six thousand people a day. No need for any software to get the account started. You can access the account from any PC with a web connection. It comes with a dictionary and a spelling checker, which is good when you are writing e-mail. Remember you want to run your business with a real professionalism.

Pronto Mail: *http://www.commtouch.com*

Juno: *http://www.juno.com*

Juno offers most of a combination of the top 2 but you have to pay $1.95 per minute for technical support. Another of the pluses is that Juno displays your mail in font and colors you prefer and it can also create multiple accounts

Of the top six companies, I like what **Bigfoot, Hotmail,** and **Juno** have to offer. The main thing for someone just starting out with a low budget is that your e-mail account is **Free** and you also get a **Free** Autoresponders with your account. I urge you to visit all 6 of the companies' sites. Everyone may have a unique situation. I combined the 2 of the top 6 accounts for their combined **Benefit**. There is that word again. Remember, only this time I was the customer.

If these Websites don't offer what you are looking for in a free e-mail program go to *http://www.emailaddresses.com*

Here you will find a list of 250 free e-mail services.

Basic Use of E-mail

When working on the Internet the standard marketing rules that are used in other media still apply. One of the basic rules is follow-up. Much of the marketing as it is done on the Internet today is what I would call single step market.

In single step marketing, you simply send one message or get one hit on your Website. You only get one chance to get your prospect buy. This kind of approach does not work well for many products on the Internet or anywhere. One-step marketing may have worked at one time when everyone lived on a farm. On a farm there was not much to do and when someone's promotional material reached you it had a high interest value. This is not true today. We are constantly being bombarded with promotional messages. It is hard to break through this promotional noise. It's often going to take at least two steps to get our prospect interested in what we have to sell.

You Need Two Steps or more on the Internet

The first thing you need to do is capture the person's e-mail address. The easiest way to do this is to offer some sort of free information or special report in your first offer. What you need to do first is have a great headline.

Autoresponder

The best way to get the report to the customer is by using an Autoresponder. An Autoresponder is an automatic e-mail reply system. You send the system an e-mail and it automatically sends back the information.

An Autoresponder allows you to have information regarding your product, service or business opportunity available 24 hours per day, 7 days per week, for anyone on the Internet or an online service such as CompuServe, AOL, Prodigy, etc. When you advertise anywhere, either online or off-line, you can always refer people to your Autoresponder address for complete details on what you have to offer. This allows anyone to get your information with a matter of minutes

Because there are many different kinds of requests that come in every day and many different replies are needed to answer these requests, you can set up many Autoresponders to provide the requested information. Even while you sleep, your post office can be a hive of activity. Receiving and sending mail all over the world. You don't have to write any letters, print reports, etc. You don't have to do a thing...it will all be taken care of for you by your Autoresponders, 24 hours a day. You can easily process over 100,000 requests daily without any effort on your part.

Here are some benefits of having Autoresponders work for you:

*Better-qualified sales leads   *Improved customer service
*Decreased postage costs   *Less information-fulfillment
                                        waste
*Increased productivity   *Higher customer satisfaction
*Faster sales generation   *Cost-effective RESULTS!!!

When you are looking for an Autoresponder keep in mind that there are a lot of different companies that offer Autoresponders. Before you go shopping around, check with your Website hosting company or Internet Service Provider. Depending on your Website hosting package that you signed up for when you signed up for your account, you may already have access to one or more Autoresponders. Each company is different, so call up your provider and check with the support staff.

For those of you who need to purchase an Auto-Responder let me tell you of one company that I have found reliable and if you decide that this will help your online business, then send me an e-mail at *bbrolhorst@wave5marketing.com*

Send This. *http://www.sendthis.com*

For $2.00 per month for each Auto-Responder you can purchase them from a company that specializes in. I have tried several different companies and have found that **Send This** Autoresponders are dependable and affordable even for the smallest marketing budget. Check out "**Send This**" Website.

Once you get your Internet business off the ground you will have customers inquiring about your products or services from around the globe. This is how the Auto-Responder works.

You place a classified ad, usually this is just a compelling short ad or headline. At the end of the ad or headline you have your Auto-Responder address. These just like an e-mail address, product@autoresponder.com. When your customers enter the e-mail address into their e-mail program, they are automatically sent a return e-mail from your Auto-Responder. It only takes a matter of seconds for them to receive the reply.

They receive an advertisement telling them in detail about your products or services that you typed and entered into your

Auto-Responder. If they require more information you can send an even more detailed advertisement. Again they access this from another of your Autoresponders.

What I like to do is to leave my Website address at the end of each bit of information in all my Auto-Responder messages. The customer can then go to my Website and see what the products or services are from a fully detailed sales letter. If they are interested they can purchase the product from my Website through a shopping cart system or by filling out a form. All this was accomplished without any physical interaction on my part.

By satisfying your prospects needs with more information you dramatically increase your percentage of sales. The key is to keep your prospect interested by pushing their hot buttons.

Your follow-up Information

How many follow up ads does it take to finalize the sale? That depends on the prospect and if you have hit their hot buttons. Most people that are marketing their products usually use just one follow up. Now let's say that there are customers like myself that have mistakenly deleted e-mail before they had a chance to read the entire e-mail ad. My point is that whoever sent me the e-mail ad, would have sent me a follow up, I would have probably bought their product because what I had read before I mistakenly deleted the e-mail I liked. Then there are some people that just need more information or more time to make a decision whether or not they want to buy a certain product or service.

If you are one of these types of marketers who like to do more than one follow up then I have a product for you. It is an Auto-Responder that can be set up to send 7 separate follow up messages. There is another advantage to using this type of

Auto-Responder. The company is **Aweber Autoresponders** *http://www.aweber.com/?17492*

You can actually make some extra money with **Aweber Autoresponders**. By becoming an associate and telling your friends and customers about **Aweber Autoresponders** you can earn a 20% commission for everyone that you send to Aweber's site to sign up for an Auto-Responder. But it doesn't stop there, for everyone that signs up for Aweber's you will earn another 10% commission for everyone that they sign up and you didn't have to lift a finger. All you have to do is put up a link on your Website and **Aweber** handles the rest. If you would like to test out one of their Autoresponders yourself go to their Website at *http://www.aweber.com/?17492*

If you are posting ads to free classified sites you may be getting certain amount of spam (unsolicited e-mail). Most of these classifieds ask for your e-mail address. Don't use your regular e-mail address. Use one of the free e-mail sites that I have listed above. I use **Bigfoot**, it has an additional surprise, free Autoresponder. So what is the big deal about **Bigfoot's** Autoresponder? From your free classified ads your **Bigfoot** address will be put on lists. Every time someone sends spam to your **Bigfoot** address they will receive your ad or sales letter telling them to go to your Website. You never know who might pick up as a customer once they get to your Website and see what products or services you offer.

For the e-mail that is redirected to your regular e-mail address you can have automatically deleted if you are using Pegasus *http://www.pegasus.usa.com/*

Or you can use Eudora Pro *http://www.eudora.com* Both of these e-mail software programs get my 2 thumbs up for filtering your incoming e-mail.

Talk about automation this is what technology can do for you. I have just sent out some classified ads, followed it up with a sales letter, got rid of my unwanted e-mail, and increased my chances of making a sale by having a merchant account to take orders from my Website. I did all this and not once talked to any-one about what I sell. You now see how all this can work for you 24 hours a day 7 days a week 365 days a year. This will work for you while you are on vacation, at one of your children's school functions, sleeping, or doing what I like to do best, golfing. So what are you waiting for?

Listed below is a number of Websites that offer Autoresponders.

http://www.infoback.net/

http://www.ourlist.net/

http://www.databack.com/mailback.htm

http://www.webthemes.com/autores.html

When purchasing an auto responder is sure to ask if the price increases if you send out 10 or 1,000. Check out the list below before you purchase an Autoresponder.

1. Are Your Messages sent directly to your e-mail address?
When you receive a response form your Auto-Responder make sure that the response is sent to your regular e-mail address

2. Getting Unlimited hits

No matter how many hits you have make sure that you are not charged extra.

3. Do you have Unlimited changes to your sales message?

Make sure that the company that you buy your Autoresponders from lets you change your inf. any time and as often as you like for no extra.

4. Number of pages in your Auto-Responder

Watch to see how many pages of text you can have. This varies from company to company

5. Logs and E-mail Information

You receive a complete log/digest of everyone (e-mail addresses) requesting your Auto-Responder.

Spambots

For those of you that have your e-mail address on your Website (if you don't you should have). There are programs called spambots. What these programs do, is go from Website to Website collecting e-mail addresses and add them to increasing lists of places to spam. There is one very effective, very easy way of protecting your site form these spambots. The program that I am referring to is called Mail Encoder *http://www.siteup.com/encoder*

Go to this Website and add your e-mail address in the requested box and you will receive a specially encoded version of your e-mail address that people can still use to contact you. This program will choke out the spambot programs and keep them from picking up your e-mail address. Make sure that you are the only one that uses the specially encoded form of your e-mail address on your Website. Believe me this program really works.

Does your E-mail Have That Professional Look?

In the Internet marketing business world e-mail is the most important means of connecting with your prospective customers, current customers, and business associates so clarity should be very important to you if you value them as customers. Before you send out any piece of e-mail you should check it for spelling and grammar. There are many good programs available that you can use that have these features. For all of my documents that I type I use Microsoft Word 2000.

Making Your E-mail Personal

Always remember that e-mail is just like a regular letter sent to your electronic mailbox. Whatever type e-mail that you send whether it is a sales letter, return mail to a prospective customer, or a message to a business associate. Try to make these types of e-mail speak directly to the reader in a personal way, much lie you would as if the person you are e-mailing was sitting right across the table from you.

When e-mail becomes impersonal it loses much of its effectiveness. If you begin your e-mail with a short personal note instead of trying to slam a sales letter right up into the readers face, your reader will feel much more at ease and be willing to read the sales letter. Not only does it help get your message read, but also it builds up a good relationship your prospects and customers. After a customer has purchased a product or service from you it is a good gesture on your part to send them a thank you note to them telling them that you really appreciate their business.

From time to time just sending them a short message to ask your customers how they are coming along with their business will bring a smile to their face and make them happy that you aren't out just to make a fast buck. When you do this it shows that you really do care about them and want them to succeed. This is why I keep a database of all my customers whether they are present or past customers. In my customer database I keep track of not only the last time I sold them a product, but also the last time I just had some contact with them. Next to their name I keep a personal record of them. What I include are their age, if they are married or single, if they have any children and what ages they are, what type of business they are in.

Chapter 7

How A Mail Managing System Can Save Time and Money

"One day, in retrospect, the years of struggle will strike you as the most beautiful."

—Sigmund Freud

Using e-mail in your marketing efforts is not only necessary it is mandatory if you want to succeed with your Internet business. As the Internet grows and the more you market your business you need something to keep your e-mail organized. With the growth of the Internet comes more software to make your business easy to run. It is becoming increasingly difficult to know what software programs to use. So how do you choose the right software? Talk with people that are Internet savvy and use their suggestions. Some may help and others may not work as well.

When you are choosing an e-mail management software package, or for that matter any type of software. You want something that is low cost or free if it is available. You also want something that is reliable, simple to use, and can save you as much time as possible.

The top three e-mail management software programs that a large part of what small Internet businesses use are:

Pegasus *http://www.pegasus.usa.com/* You can download a free version of Pegasus an their Website.

Eudora Light is a free version *http://eudora.qualcomm.com/eudoralight/*

Eudora Pro sells for $29.00. *http://eudora.qualcomm.com/pro_email3/*

Depending on your budget you can download the free versions or spend the money and get Eudora Pro. Whichever one you choose they are all excellent products that will save you both time and money.

I will go into detail about the pros and cons of each piece of software. Depending on your situation you can decide which one would work best for you.

What I mainly use software like Pegasus and Eudora for is in conjunction with my classified advertising or for customers that wants more information than my sales letters or Website could give them about my products. In other words I use it strictly for sales.

Before I go any farther let me touch on the importance of backing up all of your information, either on the hard drive or disk. In fact, I highly recommend you do both. If you were to lose all of the information, would you be able to continue with your business? I know for a fact that I couldn't.

When sending e-mail with any mail management system know that you can use it properly. Many times when I have e-mail coming in on my **AOL** account and the piece of mail was sent to sent to more than one person I can see the other peoples e-mail address. My advice to you is stay away from that. When you are sending out multiple e-mails all at the same time be sure to use the **BBC** (blind carbon copy) and not the **CC** (carbon copy) By using the **BBC** your recipients will only see their own e-mail address.

With the amount of Spam (unrequested e-mail) out there people don't need more because someone forgot to use the BBC. Not only will you keep them happy by using the BBC but also you will keep them as customers.

When someone gives me something as confidential as their e-mail address, I let them know right away that their e-mail address is safe with me and that it will not be sent out to any other of my associates or anyone else that I am contact with. Now you understand why you should never use **CC** unless what you e-mail is to people that interact with each other.

The reason I first used the **BBC** was when I had a small customer database. When I wanted to send out messages I would use my database program (Microsoft Access) and I would copy and paste their e-mail address into the **BBC**. Then I started to use the address book feature of the program. These were OK when my database was small, but as my business grew using those methods became very time consuming. Now if you are just starting out those methods are going to be just fine.

Eudora's first product "Eudora Light" went over like gangbusters and still is used heavily by new Internet business people. Mainly because of the fact that it is free. After Eudora Light had been on the market for awhile they upgraded it to Eudora Pro. Why would I want to BUY Eudora Pro when I can get Light for free? Eudora Pro has a lot more powerful features, and you get 90 days of direct telephone tech support. Try the 30-day demo free and see for yourself!

Eudora Pro was much better and its earlier counter part (Eudora Light). But when Pegasus came out I looked at both Eudora Pro and Pegasus. Both seemed to have about the same features, and both worked better than Eudora Light did. But Pegasus does have some features that neither of the Eudora versions have.

If you are currently using another software, take the time to download one or both software programs (they both are free for 30 days) and compare it to Pegasus and Eudora Pro.

Filters are a big plus when choosing an email program. What are filters? They let you automate when you are processing you e-mail. When certain words or phrases that you specify are found in the headline, subject box, or body text of your e-mail.

What Pegasus and Eudora allow you to do automatically is:

- **Forward Messages to other e-mail addresses**
- **Make messages standout by highlighting or flagging them**
- **Make copies of messages**
- **Move messages to pre-designated folders**
- **Delete messages, such as spam e-mail from certain domains**
- **Create multiple SIG files**

Both Pegasus and Eudora allow you to set up multiple SIG files and easily select any of them to be included with any given message.

Here are some of the features that Pegasus surpasses the Eudora versions. Pegasus allows people to automatically subscribe or unsubscribe their e-mail addresses from your distribution list. This feature is a necessity if you are sending out newsletters or product updates. To utilize the subscribe-unsubscribe filter it must be typed correctly by the sender, if it is not they will keep receiving the updates or newsletters. So a short note when you send it out will be helpful and eliminate unwanted e-mail. Another way around this problem is to set up a hyper link in your e-mail or Website. A hyperlink is a word that has your Website or e-mail address embedded in it. By doing this it is very easy for people with e-mail programs to that display interactive links. All the other has to do is click on the word and they will automatically be deleted from your list. In this case it would be to subscribe or unsubscribe. You can tell if it is a hyper link by the color of the word. They are a light blue color. Don't change the color as blue is the standard color for hyperlinks. By changing the color you will only confuse the people that are trying to subscribe or unsubscribe from your list.

That is one of the only differences that I can see in the difference between the two programs, but I am sure Eudora will be changing that soon. This the fastest way that I know of in setting up a filter in Eudora:

1. **Right click your mouse button on the message button**
2. **Select: make a filter**
3. **When the dialog box appears, click on the button for "create filter"**

Or You Can Do It This Way

1. **Click on the button that says, "transfer to existing mailbox" When you click on this button a menu pops up showing your folder system.**
2. **Select the mailbox you want to filter your message to.**
3. **Click the "make filter" button.**

As of this writing Eudora's Version 4.1 was in the beta stages you can download and try it for free until the real version comes out.

Chapter 8

Why You Need A Good Database Program

"You can do very little with faith, but you can do nothing without it."

—Samuel Butler

Data base programs can be useful in many ways. You can keep track of who your customers are, where they live, their phone numbers, addresses, when they bought your products, what products or services they bought, when was the last time they purchased last from you. Basically it is your customers life history.

A database is essential to keep your business alive. After you have went through all the work of attracting your new customers and sold them your initial product you want to keep them informed of new products that become available.

The key to any business is the first sale you make, but where you make your money is on return client sales. Most marketing experts will tell you that you should start off with a lower price product, a free product, or sample to draw your customers in for the higher priced items. That is where a database goes to work for you and keeps your work at a minimum.

I would have only half my business if I didn't use a database. What does it cost me for this additional business? Not a penny if I use a free database program. If I did use a database that cost me money it would still be well worth it.

Implementing a follow up from my database can substantially increase my business volume. Because follow up is so inexpensive, the business it produces is very profitable. I use a program called Access, from Microsoft Office. Any good database program will work for you.

How often do you spend frustrating time looking for an illusive piece of information you downloaded or the notes you made last year relating to something you would like to re-read to refresh your memory? Can't find them, right? We're all getting to the point of having needed information scattered all over our computer systems with no retrieval method other than searching file by file because we don't remember the file names. We all need an information management system these days that is easy, yet thorough. There are many personal information management systems available; there are several top-of-the-line database programs you could buy. Aside from Microsoft Access, which is somewhat costly, I would think seriously about trying AskSam. Here is a free version of a good data base program:

AskSam 3.0 Working Model

Download a FREE copy of askSam's Working Model check out there Website:

- *http://www.asksam.com/*

The askSam Working model comes with sample databases and lets you create your own. The Demo Version is about 2.5 MB and includes documentation. It runs on Windows 3.1, Windows 95, Windows NT, and as a Windows application under OS/2.

The Working Model gives you access to askSam's features with the following limitations:

- You cannot add or import more than 30 documents into a database (the full version has no limit on the number of documents that you can add).
- If you open a sample database containing more than 30 documents, you will not be able to edit it.
- The size of the individual documents in a database is restricted to 500 lines (the full version allows up to 16,000 lines per document).

Small Businesses / Home Offices

For office and contact management, market research databases. The askSam Office (new with version 3.0) includes easy-to-use pre-defined templates designed for addresses, notes, to do lists, faxes, memos and letters. It allows you to rapidly create interactive databases without any hassles. With its robust, comprehensive and visually pleasing interface you will be creating your first database in a flash. For Windows 95 and NT 4.0

Instabase was created with one thing in mind—simplicity.

Geared towards the non-professionals out there that just need a simple to use but powerful database, your databases and address books will be up and running in seconds!
Here's a full list of all the features you will find in Instabase:

- **Simple and easy to use interface**

Instabase uses a very simple layout making it easy to understand and use. There is no guesswork involved—you just enter your information in the pre-determined fields, save your record and proceed to the next.

- **Database Importing and Exporting**

Easily Import and Export your existing data to and from most database software.
Unlimited number of records, addresses and databases

- **Handy Toolbox**

Including links to Calculator, Phone Dialer, Paint Program and a bonus Mortgage/Loan Calculator.

- **Direct image Import/Export and Zoom function**

Add an image to every record with a simple cut & paste or import function that you can easily zoom in or open directly into MS Paint. Bookmark this feature!

- **Import and Export your comments text to Word**

We have even included an unlimited size Comments field (exportable to Word) for those long product descriptions or customer information you may have.

- **Generate detailed reports**

Easily create reports in three formats, including direct output into Excel.

Full Searching, Reporting and Address Book Sorting by any field E-mail and Internet address recognition with Internet Browser selection option (Netscape and Explorer

Chapter 9

How To Make Free Money From Your Website

"To believe in something, and not to live it, is dishonest."

—M.K. Ghandi

I know this sounds too good to be true and this goes against everything your parents told you. But in this case nothing can be closer to the truth. Making free money by the use of Affiliate programs is a good way for you to supplement your Internet income. Affiliate programs will offer your customers related products or services that will be beneficial to them as well as you.

What is an affiliate program? Affiliate programs are revenue sharing transactions organized by companies selling products or services. Website owners are paid for sending customers to the affiliates Website through a link or graphic located on your Website. They are also known as associate, re-seller, or partnership programs. Good affiliate programs will make you money as well as adding value to your site. All this is done absolutely **FREE.**

There are two ways to earn money with an affiliate program. You either join one or offer one yourself. By offering one yourself you offer other people to sell your product or service for you from their Website. (This is like advertising your product or service). First, about joining an affiliate program. Affiliates are often easy to join. After carefully reading the stipulations and conditions, which change from affiliate to affiliate, you provide a banner ad, which consists of a small graphic or ordinary link from your site or newsletter to the merchant. If someone follows the link and actually purchases a product or service from the merchant's site, you receive a commission. If you already have a busy site and the product is attractive to your visitors, it's easy to make money with no effort on your part.

The # 3 Most Important Questions To Ask
When Joining an Affiliate Program

Question # 1)

How am I paid? What is the percentage I am paid for the price of the product or service, and how is it tracked. Is it a one-time buy or is it something that is purchased every month. I prefer the monthly purchases because of the residual income, unless the product or service has a high commission and covers a wide market.

Question # 2)

How is it marketed from the company? What do they offer me, the affiliate to market their product or service such as a banner ad, referral link, or a Webpage?

Question # 3)

How does the product or service fit in with what I am marketing from my Website? Is it competitive with what I sell or does it compliment what I sell? I prefer an item that compliments what I sell.

Commissions vary from company to company. They range from as little as 5% up to as high as 15%, depending on volume of sales. I have even seen commissions as high as 25%. How many of these associate sites are making good money? Not many! These sites are either making a lot of money or hardly anything at all.

Does the Affiliate Company Compliment What You Sell?

It takes work to bring these people to your site. You have to bring them to your Website and offer them a good reason to follow a link from your Website to the affiliate you are associated with. But if you play your cards right it may not seem as difficult as I stated.

Just for example if I were selling baby cribs I could join up with a company like Amazon Bookstore and sell related books from my Website. They could be books with titles like "What to look for when buying a baby crib "or" Baby Crib Safety. These would be books that your customers would be interested in if they were in the market for one of your baby cribs. If Amazon has books with these titles you could display them on your Website by use of graphics. All your customers would have to do is click on the graphic, by doing this it would take them to the Amazon Website. If your customers buy the book you could be credited with a 15% commission. Wasn't that simple, and you had to do no work for this. They could even purchase these books as you are sleeping or on vacation.

Ask For Testimonials

Before you sign up with a company call them up or e-mail them and ask for testimonials from people that are associates, ask for names, addresses, and phone numbers. If they are legitimate they won't mind giving you this information. Just because a company doesn't give out the things listed above doesn't mean they are not on the level. But I would be leery if they don't. If the company is slow in responding to your e-mail, or phone calls that's also a warning sign. I've found that the most successful companies that I have questioned are often remarkably quick at responding to your e-mail or phone call. Read the fine print before you commit yourself.

Have You Used the Product or Service?

Never offer a product or service that you have not used yourself. If it turns out to be something that doesn't work or that you yourself was not happy with then you definitely would not want to recommend it to your customers. Things like this can back fire on you and ruin your own business. If you have tried it and it worked OK for you then you suddenly have become the expert. For an example if it were a piece of software that you bought yourself and used you would know how it works. If your customers purchased the same piece of software and were having trouble they may contact you and ask for your opinion. So always be truthful.

How To Be Successful With Your Associate Program

If you don't have your own newsletter, now is the time to get started. It's a great promotional tool I use and strongly recommend.

A great way to advertise your own products as well as your affiliate programs. If you publish your own the advertising is Free. You can also use the classifieds.

Successful associates don't just sign up for a program. Just as you would with your own products, write a summary on your Website that explains the benefits of the product or service.

If you have a new Website with low-traffic you have a lot of work ahead of you, but no need to despair. Even if your site is low on traffic you still will be able to make money. Let me tell you about some of the top affiliate programs and how they can work for you. Some companies pay you only after you have accumulated $50.00 to $100.00 in commission. If you have a very busy site, then you won't have to worry about the length of time before you get a commission check. For a small site without much traffic, it could take two or three months.

TIPS FOR AN EFFECTIVE ASSOCIATE PROGRAM

If you start such a program make sure you have lots of tools for your associates to use. Banners, pre written text for promotional mentions, pre written classified ads, and an effective tested Website they can use with secure ordering are a must. It is your responsibility to create good tools so that your associates can effectively promote, promote and promote. Make sure your program offers on line stats so your affiliates can measure the success of their efforts and track their sales. Get a program that sends them an email when a sale is made and contact your associates with new ideas regularly so they don't lose interest. Most associate programs fall flat in this area. Don't just sign them up and forget them. You are the team leader, help them succeed.

Most importantly, be generous with your commissions. Some programs are so tightfisted with their commissions; I don't know why anyone signs up. I pay a 30% referral fee to my associates. After all, without their help there wouldn't have even been a sale!

Tracking Your Affiliate

Most companies do their own tracking so you don't have to. This determines how you get paid. There is a company by the name of **LinkShare** *http://www.linkshare.com* . They are a one-stop shop for displaying your stats.

LinkShare provides you with one simple interface to participate in a number of different affiliate programs. Save time by logging in only once to check all your statistics on a near real-time basis for each merchant program. You no longer have to register with a bookseller to sell books, and then register again with a music site to sell CDs. As a LinkShare member, you can sign up for as many merchant affiliate programs as you wish. You will also have access to monthly statements and reports that detail impressions, click-through, sales, and commissions that you have generated for each affiliate program in which you are participating.

Expanding Your Business by Offering
Your Own Affiliate Program

If you want to set up an affiliate program, you have several options to choose from. You can hire a company such as AffiliateZone, which will put software on your server. You can use a shopping cart or you can write your own script *http://www.associateprograms.com/*

Affiliate Link software from AffiliateZone.com is a budget-priced option. Affiliate Link is a series of CGI scripts which allows a Webmaster to start and maintain his own affiliate program for goods or services. AffiliateZone.com will install these scripts on your server and give you some simple directions on how to use the software. You don't have to be a programmer. The merchant can choose to pay a fixed amount for click-through or set the program to pay a percentage of the goods sold, or a mixture of the two. Real-time statistics are provided so the merchant always knows who are selling what and how much, and the affiliates have peace of mind that they are not being cheated.

One of the most successful methods of marketing on the Internet is to offer people a chance to share in the profits through associate referral commissions. This is a simple way to leverage the efforts of hundreds or even thousands of people. People who advertise your products and you don't pay anything for the advertising until it results in sales!

Paul is offering you the same software he created for his own use—so you can have your OWN associate program, for any number of products! This site will tell you about the features/benefits of the software, and will also allow you to "try it out" from the perspective of your new associates, your customers, and YOU, the associates program owner! If you have any questions, please send him an email! Paul Galloway paulg@palis.com and tell him Bob Brolhorst from Wave 5 Marketing sent you. Or visit his web site: *http://www.palis.com/new/yoap10/index.htm*
http://www.palis.com/new/yoap10/index.htm for a **FREE** Demo

Associate Statistics Checking

Anytime your associates want to, they can look up the "statistics" for their web site, including orders, commissions, how many people visited, and what Internet locations they used. When it comes time for you to send commission checks to your associates, you just print out the commission data for the previous month and send it along with the check! Simple!

Paul Galloway can supply you with everything you need to start your own associate or affiliate program. A complete software package which includes a new associate "sign-up" and automatic web site replication program, an "Order Processing" program (with credit card syntax checking). As well as administrative functions, including monthly/yearly commission reports, instant associate web site updating, associate record maintenance, and more. Check out Paul's Website at *http://www.palis.com/yoap/insig.htm*

When someone signs up to be an associate, the software does the following:

1. *Creates a web site for the new associate*
2. *Notifies the new associate of their associate number, password, and web site address.*
3. *Saves the new associate's contact information for your future use.*
4. *Sends this same information in an email to the new associate.*
5. *Sends all the new associate information to you in an email.*

Once the above process is completed (it takes just seconds), the new associate can start advertising immediately!

New Orders

When an order is received from an associate's page, the following steps are taken:

1. The order form is checked making all the required information is present.
2. If a credit card is required, the number is checked for validity.

3. If there is missing information, the customer is asked to complete the missing fields and resubmit the order.
4. If all required information is present, the process continues.
5. You can hire a service such as:

Safe-Audit *http://www.safe-audit.com/*
ClickTrade *http://www.clicktrade.com/*
which can handle the money.
LinkShare at *http://www.linkshare.com*

Let GoldRush Tracking arrange the details

Since January 1998 GoldRush Affiliate Tracking Systems has offered online retail stores "everything necessary to easily build, manage and track an affiliate network". Check out their Website at *http://www.getequipped.com/*

Chapter 10

How To Use Links To Promote You're Online Business

"Service to others is the rent you pay for your room here on earth"

— Mohammed Ali

Hyper links are a free way to promote your online business by exchanging links with other related or unrelated Websites. Let me explain what a hyperlink is and what it does. A hyperlink is a special area on a Web page, which can be activated (usually with a mouse). The hyperlink can appear as text or graphic. Graphic hyperlinks work the same, as text hyperlinks except they don't change color after you have visited the site. Most hyperlinks take you to another one of your own Webpages or another Website. Other hyperlinks perform special functions, such as sending E-mail, submitting a form, accessing an ftp site, executes a database query, or accesses a discussion group.

Every browser has a function, which backs up to the previous page. In *Netscape Navigator and Internet Explorer* you press a button with a left arrow. Therefore, you can explore into the detail of a hyperlink and later return to the page that referred you there. Links are what make the World Wide Web a web.

How Do You Make A Hyperlink

For those of you just first starting out you may be wondering how you get them on your Website? They can be entered into any page or paragraph on your Website by using the text editor for your particular Website building software. What a link is actually your URL (Website address) such as mine:
http://www.wave5marketing.com
You can have your Link inserted on your Website by using the links option on your Website text editor. It can read just as mine appeared above or you can have it connected to any word or image you choose.

For example if I am trying to sell a product such as vitamins, I could use the word vitamins as a link from some-mail I sent or on a different page in my Website. To conform with the Internet community links should be highlighted in the light color of blue. By using a different color you may confuse people or they may miss your link word when reading an article that could lead them to your Website. So stick with the color blue.

By clicking on your URL or your link word with the left mouse button it will automatically take you to the site that was initiated when you produced the link. One of the two major keys to utilizing a hyperlink is use it as a guide through your own Website. The other key is to trade links with other Websites to bring your Website maximum exposure. I like to trade links with people that I do business with, not only is it beneficial to me but to them as well. The higher traffic volume site you link to the more traffic you will receive.

Now if you're just starting out that may be difficult. People may think exchanging links is a way for equal traffic, this is rare. As far as I am concerned, it makes little difference. I consider this a freebie and whomever's site I link to it will bring me more exposure and the other site more credibility.

We all have to remember that we were little guys once. Basically what we are doing is building our own community on the Internet, just as businesses in your local downtown shopping area work side by side. Usually if you see a McDonald's restaurant you will see a Burger King. Competition is the same on the Internet. Usually when a person buys a "Big Mac" from McDonald's, and like the taste they keep coming back. Just like your business on the Internet if you offer some of benefit to your prospects and they like it they will be back.

Is It A Good Idea to Link with Any Website?

Try to keep your links to sites that are related to your own. If you sold nuts and bolts you definitely would not want to link to a woman's cosmetic Website. There is nothing the two sites have in common. In fact some of your customers may be wondering what type of Website you really are running. A good rule of thumb is stay within your target market resides and does business. Depending on the size of your Website you don't want to overload your site with links and make it look like the classified ad section of your local newspaper. Remember the reason you want people to come to your Website is to purchase your products or services. So keep the external links to one a page.

Should I Trade Links With My Competitors?

Just an example, if I am to busy with some of my other duties and some requests to have a Website built, I have a link to some of my competition. The way this works is it helps me out because I don't have the time. It helps my competition out because it gives them more business. Most of all it helps my customers and gets them what they want as quickly as possible. Everybody is happy. I exchange links with a fine lady that I do business with over the Internet. Her name is LaDonna Wieland, *OffOrgnzer@aol.com*. Her Website address is *http://www.adlistings.com/office*.

What does LaDonna do as an office organizer? She proofreads anything from sales letters to things like my home study course. She is very knowledgeable in many Microsoft software uses.

LaDonna also offers services to all companies with secretarial services ranging from word processing to resume preparation. Desktop publishing of newsletters, advertising flyers or information flyers, postcards, thank you or invitations, and more. In fact she help publish this home study course for me but she does many more things of which I am not an expert on. Check out her Website at the URL above.

Andrea Smith with Adlistings Web Services is another business associate I exchange links with *http://www.adlistings.com/hosting*. Even though I build Websites myself, Andrea takes care of my overflow. Andrea and her staff are committed to superior customer service and support. They offer toll-free phone support for their clients. They not only help their clients achieve and maintain an excellent and inexpensive web presence but they also try to educate and assist their customers with any needs or questions they may have. Call them at **1-888-311-9116.**

These are just two of the many companies that I have exchanged links with. Because of the work they have done for me. I feel more than comfortable that they will offer the same to the customers that visit my Website and then link to theirs. By linking to both of our sites the customer will have a chance to visit both sites and will be able to see what we both offer. If they like what they see we both have customers for life as long as we keep fulfilling our customers needs. All this was accomplished by a simple link that cost both my competitor and myself nothing.

How to Check Your Links

Once you have been in business for a while, and your business expands, the more links you will have. Some of these you may forget you have. So when you get to that point or even if you are just starting out, let me recommend a couple of Websites and services that is a must to have.

The utility is called Submit Plus *http://www.submitplus.com/sitetest.htm* Up until a couple of months ago I was keeping my own directory for my external links, but it was very time consuming. I used "Microsoft Access" to keep the database of links I have, but don't get me wrong that was a great piece of software to use and I still use it for my customers database. That's when I came across Submit Plus, I am always looking for a way to save myself time and money if possible.

This utility will keep and manage my directory of links located on the jumplist database on their server. You use a form setup by Submit Plus and enter all your information, submit it, and jumplist will maintain the directory of links for you. Here's the kicker; Submit Plus is FREE so you can try it first to see if it will work for you. Jumplist offers a single category that will take up to 100 links. If you have more than that, then they offer a larger version with multiple categories. Each category will hold 999 links with a price of $30.00 per year.

This program is well worth the money for the amount of time it will save you. But hold on there is more! It will also check your links to see if they are still active and if they are not you will receive an e-mail from Submit Plus stating which links are no longer active or are broken. You can even have it setup for visitors to add links to your database as well. If you belong to a Network Marketing company and have many people in your downline or upline you could use the list for all of your distributors if you purchase the commercial version you have access to some tools that could be very useful to you.

Here is another site that I ran across that offers somewhat the same service: *http://www.linkalarm.com/testdrive/?358097732* LinkAlarm checks every page below this URL. You can check http://www.host.com just a directory *http://www.host.com/site* or just one page *http://www.host.com/site/page.html*

Take their free test drive now! You'll be a fully-fledged LinkAlarm member for 2 months free of charge. Just fill in the form at the Website. The Free 2-Month test-drive, no cost, and no obligation. You can't lose. Just fill in the form at their Website and they will get to work.

If LinkAlarm doesn't help congratulations, you manage your web site better than most. If it does, become a member for 12 months (only $20 for 200 pages) and LinkAlarm will report to you punctually, accurately and informatively every month.

Since we are the subject of link programs, let me throw one more at you *http://www.cyberspyder.com/*. I don't know a lot about the software but thought if anyone was interested they could check it out. Broken links a problem? Try the user friendly Cyberspyder Link Test Version 2.1.4

CyberSpyder Link Test is a Web site management program to be used for verifying that the URL's on a site are not broken and for analyzing site content. It is designed for sites of all sizes.

From the very small personal or business Web site with only a few pages, to the very large corporate site with thousands of links.

The program includes features found in more expensive programs, but at a price affordable by the owner of a small personal site. The program is distributed as shareware, and may be used free for up to 60 days for evaluation purposes. Registration is $35.00 if you decide to keep the program.

This goes a little bit away from the links subject but I came to my mind when I was talking about software and links. If you want to know where people came from that visited your Website and what keywords were used to find your site. Then I suggest that you try this **FREE** tracking utility at
http://www.extreme-dm.com/tracking

Chapter 11

How to Increase Your

Sales and Find Your Target Market
"You cannot tell your heart what it wants. Your heart will tell you."

—Barbara Sherman

There are two surveys that I am going to discuss. Both are completely different from each other, yet bring the same results. Finding one effective way to gather customer information is to insert a questionnaire into your web site. You are giving your customers a choice as to what kind of products or service that they would like to see developed.

Most people will open up to you if they see you are running a survey, especially when you have products or services that they think will be helpful to them. Many people are some what addicted to answering survey questions, so you will receive some responses immediately just out of others curiosity.

There are a couple of ways to promote your survey. One is to leave a message at the bottom of your questionnaire, let people know that after they have taken the survey to be sure to tell their friends and business associates. The other when you do your follow up with those who filled out your survey, leave a message stating the same thing you did on your Website and to thank them for completing it.

Always ask people to bookmark your Website. This what is commonly known as a call to action, people liked to be helped out and when you are asking them to bookmark your site you are doing them a courtesy. The next time they want to look for your site they will remember the bookmark. Don't expect people to do the unexpected. Unless you guide them along the way, and ask them do to do something, they won't. Once you have your survey up and running on your Website you can change it at any time. Why change it, it allows your customers to know that your listening to their views and your willingness to give them what they ask for.

Just like the rest of your Website, you should test out your survey or have someone else test it out to make sure it is working properly. By working properly I mean make sure that when a person types in a response to your survey questions that you are receiving the response. A survey that does not work properly is one of the annoying things that a future prospect won't even bother with. If it doesn't work the first time they are more than likely to leave the Website. This can also be a bad reflection on your business and bad news travels fast.

Here are some of the things that have happened to me when I participated in someone else's surveys. I went to the trouble of filling out a lengthy survey, mainly because I like some of the beginning questions. When I am done I push the submit button, nothing happens! Do you think I will go back and fill out the survey again? I don't think so. That person just lost a potential sale. Do you see now why you want a fully functional survey?

If your survey is to reach just a few hundred prospects, you may decide to send it out via your e-mail software. If you are sending it out to a larger group of people, lets say in the tens of thousands to hundred of thousands of prospects, you need a more vigorous and efficient device. There are services on the Internet that offer survey distribution by way of e-mail Check out the information at this site *http://webcommunique.cetiinc.com/*.

Their service creates unique URL's based of the prospect's e-mail address and your e-mail survey page so the identity of the prospect is already known as they complete the survey. This allows Webmasters to associate e-mail addresses with survey responses without having to ask the identity of that visitor. This is something that a prospect may be unwilling to do because of the privacy issue. What Ceti does is supply you important information on what your prospects needs are from the survey they filled out as well as their e-mail address.

When you are done setting up your survey make sure there is some sort of benefit that the prospect will get by filling out the survey. It doesn't have to be a freebie, although that is what I like to send them. I usually send a **FREE** report; these have worked well for me in the past. Not only are they getting something free but also I am further promoting the times that I offer. These free reports are not only easy to write but they give you credibility. After your prospects have filled out the survey ask them if they would mind receiving future information in their areas of interest.

9 Survey Secrets That You Should Collect

Here is what I use when I want to improve everything that I market from my home study course to my Website or even the survey they are filling out.

1. *What readers like or dislike about your survey.*
2. *If people didn't fill out your survey what type of survey would they look for?*
3. *What is the price range that they are looking for?*
4. *What type of information are they looking most for?*
5. *If they are buying a product or service how to make purchasing that product easier; i.e. credit card, check by fax or phone.*
6. *Website information: Asking your prospects how you can improve your Website to include items of interest to them.*
7. *Demographic information: Tell your prospects that not every question has to have an answer. If they offer just a few answers you have something to build a business relationship on. Don't be too aggressive.*
8. *If they do give you an e-mail address tell them that they do not have to worry their e-mail address is safe with you and that it won't be traded or sold to anyone.*
9. *Be careful what you ask for. Prophesies have a way of fulfilling themselves but the answers to your questions often don't. Only ask the questions that are necessary to add value to your survey you will experience dismal results if you ask nonessential or overly deceitful questions.*

The other survey are not surveys that you conduct but by an outside service. A company called GVU website address: *http://www.nua.ie/surveys/* Gvu has thousands of surveys that they run throughout the year. You're asking how does this help me? It can help you develop new products or services depending on the survey's results.

What Products Should I Offer

Books were the most popular item, followed by computer hardware and computer software. 5.6 million people purchased a book online, representing an increase of 3.3 million. 4.4 million people purchased computer hardware, up 2.4 million, and 4 million online consumers purchased software, up 1.2 million from September 1997. There was also a significant increase in the number of people making travel purchases, up 1.6 million to 2.8 million, and clothing purchases were up 1.8 million to 2.7 million people.

Using these surveys you can plan on what to write reports on. If you sell informational products that can be published in online areas like America Online for free. Why would you want to do this? It is another way to attract new prospects to your Website. Where on **AOL** can I display these reports? Any of **AOL's** business libraries are great places to post a report or article. Publishing articles in areas like this will expose you to a larger community of interested people. Posting these articles or reports will also allow you to be looked upon as an expert in your field as well as gaining credibility. If your articles are well written and have good content, **AOL**, magazines, and newsletters may want to publish your articles or reports.

The main purpose of this survey is to understand how customers treat Customer Satisfaction surveys. If you have participated in any Customer Satisfaction survey in the past, please take a couple of minutes to answer this very short survey. All information you provide will be kept absolutely confidential and used only in terms of statistics. Upon completing the survey, you will receive an exclusive report on this survey. Below is a sample of a survey that I have sent out. What it does is it gives me a general idea of how my customers perceive my business, and what if any changes I can make in my marketing.

1. **What was your answer to a question like 'overall, how are you satisfied with the company?**
   1. 'Very satisfied'
   2. 'Somewhat satisfied'
   3. 'Not satisfied/not dissatisfied'
   4. 'Somewhat dissatisfied'
   5. 'Very dissatisfied'
   6. 'Don't know' or did not answer

2. **If your answer to that question was 'very satisfied', why were you 'very satisfied'?**
   1. I did not have any problems with the company's services/products.
   2. I had problems but the company resolved them to my satisfaction
   3. The company's performance exceeded my expectation
   4. The company's performance was of the best
   5. There was no room for further improvement
   6. I was not dissatisfied
   7. I made comparisons and found its service/product was superior
   8. Other (please specify):

3. **If your answer to that question was 'very dissatisfied', why were you 'very dissatisfied'?**
   1. I had problems with the company's services/products
   2. I had problems but the company could not resolve them to my satisfaction
   3. The company's performance was short of my expectation
   4. The company's performance was not the best
   5. There was plenty room for the company to improve its performance
   6. I was not satisfied
   7. I made comparisons and found its service/product was inferior
   8. Other (please specify):

4. **What was your answer to a question like 'how likely are you to maintain your relationship with the company?**
    1. *'Very likely'*
    2. *'Somewhat likely'*
    3. *'Not likely/not unlikely'*
    4. *'Somewhat unlikely'*
    5. *'Very unlikely'*
    6. *'Don't know' or did not answer*

5. **If your answer to that question was 'very likely', how serious are you to commit your answer?**

Very serious   Not serious at all
<—— 5   4   3   2   1 ——>
5 4 3 2 1
Your choice
If your answer to that question was 'very unlikely', how serious are you to commit your answer?

Very serious   Not serious at all
<—— 5   4   3   2   1 ——>
5 4 3 2 1

Your choice

7. *Do you still maintain a good relationship with that company?*
    1. *Yes*
    2. *No*

8. *How are you satisfied with the following aspects of your most recent customer satisfaction survey?*

Very satisfied   *Very dissatisfied*
<——— 5   4   3   2   1 ———>
5 4 3 2 1

Questions asked in the survey
Time taken to answer the survey
Feedback of your concerns
Improvement on what you were dissatisfied
The purpose of the survey

9. Overall, how are you satisfied with your most recent customer satisfaction survey?
1. *Very satisfied*
2. *Somewhat satisfied*
3. *Not satisfied/not dissatisfied*
4. *Somewhat dissatisfied*
5. *Very dissatisfied*

10. How do you agree with the following statements?
Strongly agree   strongly disagree
<——— 5   4   3   2   1 ———>

After a customer satisfaction survey, I feel I have a closer relationship with the company.

I never took a customer satisfaction survey seriously.

I felt the company cares about its customers.

From the survey, I think the company doesn't really understand what a customer needs.

The company takes my answers seriously.

The company should have a better way (than a customer satisfaction survey) to understand its customers' needs.

The company is making efforts to improve what I was dissatisfied.

The company seems to concern more about its profits than about my satisfactions.

If I am surveyed again by the same company, my attitudes will be more positive.

After each Category it is suggested that you leave a comment box to give your prospects the opportunity to give you comments regarding the question.

Surveys can be obtained from your Web hosting Company. Call up customer support, they will be more than happy to help you. Or checkout the Website listed below.

http://www.virtua.com/fastvote/

FastVote is the first Java product to provide Webmasters worldwide with a configurable and simple way to poll users. The system allows Webmasters to quickly and easily creates and deploys new surveys on the fly, eliminating the need to write custom scripts for each and every poll. All results are instantly available and stored for later reference. FastVote is perfect for everything from internal corporate, university, and government surveys (within Intranets), kiosks, and high-volume surveys and polls on national and international web sites

Your business will be sure to grow and your customers will appreciate and respect you for your willingness to put up a survey to help them.

Chapter 12

How to Increase Your Sales by As Much As 85%

"Accept the challenges so that you can feel the exhilaration of victory."

—General George S. Patton

Before I really get into the basics of setting up a merchant account, you need to know that there is a new company online that eliminates the high cost of setting up a merchant account. Read what some of the major publications are saying:
CNET Recommends

PayPal **http://www.cnet.com/internet/0-3761-7-2040210.html?st.cn.3761-7-2040212.ss.3761-7-2040210**
PayPal's the most reliable personal bill payment service on the Web. It's easy to use, offers a convenient auction payment form, and delivers your dough faster than most of the other services we reviewed. Plus, it lets you beam funds to your buddies via Palm

handheld devices. On the downside, PayPal won't send money to a recipient's credit card and takes a week or two to get money to folks who don't have checking accounts. But overall, we think PayPal offers the best combination of speed, security, and features. And best of all, it's free.

If you sell products or services online then PayPal is for you or any business online. Its FREE and very reliable and PayPal even gives you $5.00 FREE just for signing up. I have used this service time and time again and without fail the money was transferred into my bank account. Check it out at: *https://secure.paypal.com/refer/pal=bbrolhorst%40wave5marketing.com*

Why do you want to accept credit cards by way of your Website? More people will buy your products. You probably already know that it's no secret, there are many reasons why more consumers are using "plastic" these days: bonus points, easier to carry, makes large purchases affordable, makes impulse buys easier.

There are many figures thrown out as to what the percentage of increased sales are by accepting credit cards online. The range is anywhere from 300% to over 800%, depending on who your target market is and what you sell. The bottom line however, is if you don't accept credit cards online you will be missing out on a huge percentage of your market. Of all the ways in which a sale can be paid for, C.O.D., money order, check by fax or phone and credit cards, credit cards make up to 80% of those sales.

Some small business owners have the idea that only big businesses are the only business that can offer payment by credit card. Well nothing could be farther from the truth. In fact because of the Internet, the price of credit card transactions has dropped considerably. Not only will accepting credit cards through your Website increase your sales, but also it will help put your business on autopilot. People will be able to buy any of your products or services that you offer from your Website by filling out a form. By the click of a button the sale will be completed and your customers should be able to receive their merchandise in as little as 24 hours of filling out the form. Accepting credit cards online is just one of many ways you can use to put your business on autopilot.

What this means is more time for you to concentrate on the things that will mean more sales for you, marketing and promoting your Website and products or services. Not only does a merchant account make life easier and create more time for you, but also it does the same for your customers. For most of your customers who will not be in your local telephone area, that want to make a purchase could be turned away for something as little as a long distance phone call.

So don't take that chance, get a merchant account now and start making money like the big businesses. Now that you see how a merchant account will help increase your sales, the next step will be to set up a merchant account for yourself. Follow my advice and I will show you how to get the biggest bang for your buck.

First of all if you have decided on a web hosting company, check and see if they offer a shopping cart system and if the software you are going to use to accept credit cards is compatible with their servers. If you are just starting out you may be in better shape because you can pick your software and then decide on your web Hosting companies and not have to worry about transferring all your Website information.

I did some extensive research on the Internet as well as offline publications such as newspapers and magazines and came up with some surprising information. What I found out was prices generally start out around $300.00 for the software and the normal merchant fees. Now these normal merchant fees can vary also, from 1.89% per transaction up to 3.50% per transaction. A two percent difference may not seem like much, but as your business grows and the more sales you make plus if you sell high dollar items this 2% difference can really add up fast, so it pays to shop around. Compare this to leasing the software and equipment you can stand to lose as much as $1400.00 dollars just by leasing and when your lease is up you have nothing to show for as far as your merchant equipment is concerned. Absolutely stay away from leasing a merchant account terminal. Most of these leases run for 48 months. These leases can run over $2400.00. Keep in mind that these leases usually run from 36 to 48 months and once you have signed a lease you are committed for that amount of time.

Compare the typical rip off processor:

$50.00 to $200.00 application fee
Lease a terminal for 48 months
$25.00 to $30.00 per month
$16.00 to $20.00 statement fee
$0.20 -$0.25 transaction fees
1.89% to 3.50% discount rate

Most small businesses just starting out can not afford expenses as large as these can, at least not until you have a larger customer base to work with. But even if you have a large customer database, why pay these higher prices. You have a few other alternatives that keep you more in line with a startup budget. One is to buy merchant account software. The other would be to go with a company like Costco. *http://www.costco.com*
1-800-220-6000

Costco is wholesale house that deals in many cost savings programs? They have one of the most economical merchant account services around the only sticker is that you have to pay a $100.00 yearly membership fee.

Here's how it stacks up
Year 1
$100.00 per year membership fee
$25.00 application fee
Terminal outright buy or rent with the option to cancel (not buy/lease)
No statement fee
No transaction fee
$2.00 discount rate
Total fixed cost Year 1 $150.00
Total fixed cost Year 2 $125.00
You can save from $500.00 to $1000.00 with Costco. Not to mention there are no transaction fees and lower discount rates.

WebGenie Shopping*CartPro, WebGenie
http://www.webgenie.com
CGIs—use on most servers
WebGenie Shopping Cart—Basic $ 295
WebGenie Shopping Cart—Professional $ 495

Hazel, Netsville $195.00
http://hazel.netsville.com

Flexibility is just one of their outstanding features. Another is their price they start at just $195.00 for a store of up to 100 products. For only $495.00, you can offer an unlimited variety and volume of products on your site. You may purchase additional options to expand and enhance the functionality of your Hazel account, as you need them.

http://www.bankcard-processing.com/

Super LOW Fixed Processing Rates of 1.45% to 1.57% (depending on the program)! NO Application Fees! NO Installation Fees! NO Training or Set-Up Fees! Programs available with GUARANTEED APPROVAL regardless of credit history! Most Programs have NO Monthly Minimum Fees and NO Annual Membership Fees! Funds deposited into your checking account within 48 hours!

Equipment available at reasonable rates–and more often than not equipment comes with a FULL LIFETIME REPLACEMENT WARRANTY!

Toll free Customer Support—24 hours a day / 365 days a year!

http://www.aismedia.com/home/e_commerce/Real_Time_Processing/I ndex.htm? **co1866xcc**

This company is new and I just ran across it on the Internet while I was researching for new merchant accounts. They offer an incredible service with fees that are some of the best on the "WWW". Plus they offer a reseller's program that pays $175.00 for each referral. They will also host your site for $16.95 per month. To inquire call **1-770-451-9499**

Service Fees
Service AIS TransAct Other Services
One Time Set-Up Fee: $50 $350.00—$699.00
Annual Fee: $0.00 $99.00—$250.00
Secure Server Access: $0.00 $19.95—$29.95 per month
Set-up time same day 3—5 days

Technical Support: 24 Technical Support varies
Cost Per Transaction: $0.00* 1—3% Per Transaction
Fixed Minimum Transaction Fee: $0.00 Fee: $0.10-$0.75 Per Transaction
Minimum Monthly Transaction Fee: $35.00 $35.00—$75.00
Total Start-Up Cost: $85.00 $350.00—$740.00

PLEASE NOTE: The fees listed here are above and beyond those charged by your credit card merchant account processor, financial institution, bank, or agency.
* First 500 transactions each month are FREE. Additional transaction is billed at $0.12 per transaction. For detailed information, see our service agreement

http://www.itransact.com/info/redicharge.html

Real-time Credit Card Verification
RediCharge is the most advanced, secure, and reliable method for accepting credit cards online. The RediCharge system enables merchants to verify and process credit card orders online in real-time. Merchants also have access to many useful interfaces, such as online manual order entry and online credits to customer accounts. ITransact's advanced technologies enable you to easily accept both checks and credit cards using your existing web site, credit card merchant account, and online order forms. Your web site can be hosted on any server without compromising the security of your customers' data.

Hassan Consulting's Shopping Cart *http://www.irata.com*
CGIs—use on most servers

Free

PerlShop
http://www.arpanet.com/perlshop
CGIs—use on most servers
Free

JSHOP
http://www.jshop.co.uk

JavaScript will work on any server, and is very easy to install. It requires no program files installed at the server, but a significant number of users have browsers that won't work with JavaScript; perhaps 20+% or more of all users are working with browsers that won't work with JavaScripts very well, or at all.

Category 3—Sign Up With a Hosting Company

Snapsite Web Architect, Media in Motion
http://www.mediainmotion.com

not yet available—probably available May/June 98 this product can only be used through a hosting company that has installed the Snapsite software.

Category 4—Use a Service
$49 for the software, then $99/mth, 2.5% per transaction
QuickSite, Site Technologies
http://www.sitetech.com

Although from the advertising one might assume that this product should be in category 1 or 2 (Site Technologies advertises that this product includes "a full suite of Internet commerce tools. Catalog Builder including OrderEasy"), I've listed the program in category 4, because the program itself has no shopping-cart capabilities. Rather, it provides an easy way to link to the OrderEasy service (listed below), and QuickSite owners get a discount at that service. You can link to other services if you prefer. $99/mth, 2.5% per transaction, $49 setup

OrderEasy
http://www.ordereasy.com
Credit-card transaction processing included $90/mth, $120 setup

DXShop
http://www.dxshop.com
$50/mth, $250 setup

The Engine, Icorp
http://www.icorp.net/engine
$119/3 months

Smart ShoppingCart, WebGenie
http://www.webgenie.com
$35/mth, $20 setup

WizzCart, Marketwizz
http://www.wizzcart.com
AUD$40/mth (Australian dollars)

Sofcom
http://www.sofcom.com.au
$249/year

Americart
http://www.cartserver.com/americart
$20/mth, $75 setup

CyberCart
http://www.lobo.net
$120/6 months

Internet Shopping Cart Server
http://www.webisland.com/cart/index.htm

Chapter 13

Bonuses and Free Reports

"The greatest thing in the world is not so much where we are, but in what direction we are moving."

—O.W. Holmes

Have you ever purchased a product or service that offered some kind of incentive or bonus, but you were more interested in the bonus? Let me explain with an example. I bought a Wilson basketball and it came with a coupon for 50% off of a pair of Converse basketball shoes. Since I coach basketball for a pee wee basketball team and I didn't really have a need for another basketball at the time but I did need a pair of basketball shoes. As it turned out it would have cost me $72.95 for the shoes and the Basketballs cost $32.95 for a total of $105.90. By getting 50% off of the shoes that total came down to $69.42

Another good example to follow is what the automobile industry does when selling their new cars. Let's say you were looking for a Ford Mustang with a convertible top. You came across one at dealer's lot but it had a cloth interior and the cloth interior was $1500.00 more. What this did was to drive up the value of that particular car, but to get the convertible you went ahead and bought it anyway even though vinyl seats would have been just as good. So what's the point in all this? What this shows is that if you package items together you can drive up the perceived value of that package thus raising your price. Now not everyone will want everything that is in the package, but if they like one or two of the items they will probably buy the package deal.

When you start marketing your products or services use the above approach to increase your sales. This is known as up selling and there are a lot of businesses that do this and do it very effectively. What I do is I take the products that I use for running my business and show my prospective customers how these products can save them time and money. I write a report on these items that I know will help my customers because they have worked for me and then I offer it as a free report or bonus. So what better way to sell a product then to offer a free bonus that is good enough to sell on its own.

How to Take a Package of Items and
Sell Them for A Higher Price than the Package Itself

Believe when I tell you that this has really increased my total profits while keeping my overhead low. Here's the way it worked for my home study course.

What I did was take every chapter in my book and by separating them and made 20 plus single reports and sold them for between $10.00—$20.00. So it brought the total perceived value up to over $500.00 dollars and that didn't include the other free things that were supplied by some of the Websites that I made reference to in the course. For instance in the course I gave my customers 250 Free places to advertise on the Internet. If you figured out what the savings was for the free classified sites the perceived value would have risen by about $2500.00 based on that if the average Internet classified charged you $100.00 per ad. As you know by now if you purchased the entire course or visited my Website at *http://www.wave5marketing.com* you know the home study course sells for $89.00.

When I constructed my Website I listed all of the chapters of my home study course separately and gave a brief description of each chapter and what they would be sold for separately. By doing this I actually increased my customer base because there were people that did not need all of the information in every chapter. So buying the separate reports actually saved some of my customers' money by buying only the information they needed.

Another group of customers, the ones that were just starting out, maybe couldn't afford the entire home study course. What it gave them was the opportunity to get their business off of the ground by buying the reports they thought could benefit them most.

The last groups of customers were the ones that could see the savings of buying the whole course even if they wouldn't use the information in every chapter. Plus after talking to them after they purchased the course, they informed me that they didn't want to miss out on the freebies that I listed through out the course. Instead of having one target group I came up with three and increased my sales over 260%. So when starting out your own business, or if you are already in business you may want to include this marketing tactic and turn some of those ideas into some cold hard cash.

Killing Two Birds with One Stone

You have written reports to sell separately but how do you advertise them? By separating these reports and by taking small portions of information and cutting and pasting them into a document I came up with a dynamite sales letter that took me all of about 2 minutes to put together. For those of you that are developing your own products whatever type of products that you sell here is a good rule of thumb as to what you should charge for them. The formula I use is to keep your head above water is charge your customers 4—5 times more for the product than what it cost you to produce.

If you are looking for products to produce find some that would be relatively inexpensive to produce and then sell them using the formula above. This known as having a high profit margin. What ever you sell or if you give away free reports make sure that even the free reports offer a benefit. Without a benefit your product is useless and more than likely you won't be in business long. Put yourself in your customer's place and ask how this free report or bonus will help? Will it save me time, save me money, make me money, improve my health, or increase my leisure time? Whatever the case, make sure it has a benefit.

Follow Up

After your product is sold or you received contact information by e-mail, phone or snail mail now is the time for your follow. A good way to improve your products or give you ideas for new ones. For those that have bought my products I like to do a follow up with them and ask them what was the main reason for them buying my product or service. For those who did not buy, if I have their contact information I want to contact them as well.

This can work out good for you in a couple of different ways. By contacting them they will be able to tell you why they didn't purchase from you. Ask them what they didn't like. This way you can get ideas on how to improve your present product or an idea for new products.

So information can help you develop products or services, it can also help you regain lost customers. The biggest reason for doing this is that you are out there to help them and that your not just someone on the Internet looking to make a fast buck.

Informational products are a big seller over the Internet and offer a high dollar value. They also don't cost a lot of money to produce. If you are just starting out in your business and you don't know what to charge for your products. A good rule to charge 4 to 5 times more than the product cost you to produce and then by offering a free bonus you would have made your offer irresistible.

Chapter 14

Search Engine Placement and Registration

"Be thankful for problems. If they were less difficult,
someone with less ability might have your job."

—Unknown

You have your Website built and you have picked out your Website host or Internet Service Provider. Whatever software you used to design your Webpage or Website it will come with a Publish or Print button. Basically this takes the pages you have designed and saves them on your computers hard drive and prints it to your web server on the World Wide Web. Pretty easy so far isn't it.

I would like to talk for a moment on the importance of getting your own personal domain name. Now this does not apply to everyone, but if you have your own company you would certainly want your domain name to reflect what kind of business you're in. For instance if you were selling antique automobile maybe something like antiqueautos.com would be appropriate. If you were in the recipe card business then something like recipes.com would work for you. In my case since I am in the business of Internet Marketing, thus *http://www.wave5marketing.com*. Remember when you type in these URL's they should be all lower case letters and no separation in-between letters.

SELECTING THE RIGHT BUSINESS NAME

Ask 100 people already in business how they decided upon their business name and you will get 100 different answers. Everyone has a story behind how he or she chose their own business name. Even if the business is named after their selves, there's a reason why this was done.

When you open a business, in a sense, you are causing a new birth. You or your associates created this new birth from an idea alone. It will have its own bank account, it's own federal identification number, it's own credit accounts, it's own income and it's own bills. On paper, it is another individual! Just as if you were choosing a name for your own unborn child, you need to spend considerable time in deciding upon your business name. There are several reasons why a good business name is vitally important to your business. The first obvious reason is because it is the initial identification to your customers. No one would want to do business with someone if they didn't have a company name yet. This makes you look like an amateur who is very unreliable. Even if you call your company **"Sally's Hair Salon"** a company name has been established and you are indeed a company. People will therefore feel more comfortable dealing with you.

Secondly, a business name normally is an indication as to the Product or service you offer. **"Ethel's Typing Service," "Karate for Kids"**

"**Joe Dandy Jack-of-all-Trades** and **"A1 Publishers"** are all examples of simple business names that immediately tell the customer **WHAT** product or service you offer. However, most people will choose the simple approach when naming a business. They use their name, their spouse's name, their children's names or a combination of these names. The national hamburger-restaurant chain **"Wendy's"** was named after the owner's daughter. However, research has proven that these "cutesy" names are not the best names to use.

Many experts claim that it makes the business look too "mom-and-pop." This depends on the business. If you are selling something that demands this mood or theme to appeal to your market, it's best to use this approach. Personally, I am inclined to name my businesses with catchy names that stick in people's heads **AFTER** we have initially made contact. Names like, **"Sensible Salads"**. This is a company that publishes diets based on eating things light like salads. **"Lawyers Lobby,"** a company that publishes newsletters for Attorneys. **"Black Ink,"** a company that sells printing supplies. **"Printer's Pals,"** a publishing company. "Strictly Obedient," a company that sells books on how to train your dog. These are all good examples of catchy names. These types of names not only relate to your product or service but also serve as a type of slogan for your business. This is a big help when marketing your business. A friend I know owns a business called **"Herbs & More."** He grows and sells his own line of raw seasonings to people in the local area. At his grand opening, he passed out his business card. The card had the scent of dill and on the back and the slogan reads: "Don't go any where else and get pickled. Buy your herbs from us." This marketing concept not only got my friend noticed and remembered but brought in several huge orders for the business.

When you name a son or daughter, you may not decide upon a definite name until after they are born. You do this because a name is sometimes associated with a type of personality. When you name a business you may need to wait until you have a product or service to sell and then decide upon a business name before going into the business itself because your business name should give some clue as to what product or service you are selling.

A business named **"Harry's Collections"** normally wouldn't sell car parts and a business named "Catchers Mitt" would not sell knitting supplies.

To generate ideas begin looking at business signs everywhere you go. Notice which ones catches your eye and stick in your mind. Try and figure out "why?" Naturally, the business **"Dominos Pizza"** sticks in your mind because it is nationally known. These don't count! Look around and notice the smaller businesses. Take your time, within a few days you should be able to come up with a few potential business names. Then, when you finally find a few names you really like try reciting them, get others opinions. It won't be long until your business will have the proper name that will carry it through its life!

MAIL ORDER HINT

Try to avoid very long names so they will fit into small display ads. **Melinda's Merry Christmas Gifts,** for example, will take up essential ad space.

But to get your own domain name first you have to see if its available through a company called Internic and if you have access to the world wide web. Then you will want to go to your web browser and type in Internic URL. This stands for Universal Resource Locator. What this is basically, is your address on the World Wide Web. If you know of a name for your business that you think would be good for what it is that conveys what type of business that you have then go to this URL: *http://www.i2000.net/*

When you get to the Website you will see a place to type in your domain name to see if it is available. If it is not it will instruct you to choose another. When you find one that is not taken you will be able to scroll down to the registration form. This is fairly self-explanatory. When I registered for my first domain name it was somewhat of a fiasco.

There were forms to fill out. Some, I had no idea how to fill them out. When I had finished I registered them online through Internic. That is when my frustration set in. To make a long story short, when I signed up with **Accesspoint** *http://www.accesspoint.com* I told them I had my own domain name but did not know how to register it. They told me they would take care of it and within a day it was done. Sometimes it is better to leave things up to the professionals.

Besides it let me do what I do best and that is teach people how to avoid these situations and get you to making money much faster.

SEARCH ENGINE LISTINGS

A Naked Truth approach to beating out your competitors Fast Easy and **FREE**. I will show you secrets of getting your site coming out on TOP of your competitors. The first step to **SUCCESSFUL SEARCH ENGINE LISTINGS**. Before you read these little **"SEARCH ENGINE SECRETS"**, about search engine listings, keep this in mind.

This is the single most important tip I can give you. **BE HONEST!** One thing, (maybe the only thing), all search engines and directories have in common is that they were all designed to give the searcher the pages it feels are most relevant to the search key words that the person doing the search enters. This is as it should be. We've all done searches for financial advice for example: Type in **STOCK MARKET** and the first 3 out of ten pages that come up is junk like " steaming hot babes that speculate". I think this is ridiculous and if you're serious about running a legitimate Internet business you'll find that you'll be much more successful by attracting people to your page that are truly interested in information about you and your product or service.

So before you begin a search engine listings anywhere, remember that you should choose the key words and keyword phrases that your customers would use to try to find an honest and respectable business page that really would provide them with the search that they are looking for. Then make your home page relevant to those key words and key word phrases.

If your site is not showing up in the top 100 search engine queries, you are missing out on thousands of hits, and that could mean thousands of dollars going to your competitors instead of going into your pockets. Surveys show that over 1,500 web pages are coming on line every day! People who learn and use these little known secrets and apply them will dramatically increase their chances of success. When it comes to Search Engine Listing, I can show you how you can be one of the best and compete with the professionals with just a few simple tasks. I have done my homework through 1000's of hours of work by researching the top major search engines and have learned many invaluable tips on winning out over our competition. Of course I'm not going to give away all my secrets, but I will share a few of the best **"Secrets of the Trade"** to help you get on top and stay there.

SECRET #1—YOUR WEBSITE TITLE:

This is what comes up first on the Search Engine so it's the first thing others will read about you. First impressions are so important. You not only want others to see your site listed, you want them to click on it and go to your site. So here is a simple little secret that works like a charm. People want information, especially **"INSIDE"** information so give them a sense that you're letting them in on something. For example: "Jon Doe's Accounting" "Instead: **HOW TO WIN THE WAR WITH THE IRS**: Accounting Tips the IRS Doesn't want you to know! Now from those 2 site titles, which one do you think you would click on? Studies show that these other words pull traffic like crazy: **" DISCOVER", "HOW YOU CAN", "SENSATIONAL" "FREE WHOLESALE KIT"**

SECRET #2—HOW TO BEAT OUT YOUR COMPETITOR WHEN HE OR SHE HAS THE SAME KEY WORDS:

Although there are hundreds of search engines, each has their own way of searching for individual Webpages. Most engines search by relevancy. In other words, the more a Website pertains to the key words or key phrases the better chance it will come up first. Try to include your key words or key phrases in your text as much as possible without being redundant. This page is a good example, how many times have you seen the phrases **"SEARCH ENGINES"** and **SEARCH ENGINE LISTINGS"**? Those are two of our key words.

SECRET #3—ANOTHER WAY TO BEAT YOUR COMPETITION WITH THE SAME KEY WORDS AND KEY PHRASES:

Many search engines use alphanumerically **"Ties"** (by your site title) to keywords. So if your site title is **"Perfumes by Sylvia"** and your competitor's site title is **"America's Hottest Selling Perfumes"** your competitor will probably come up first. It's a good idea to try to name your site with a number (#1) or the letter "A "to give you another little edge.

SECRET #4—KEY WORDS AND KEY PHRASES:

The thing to remember about key words and key phrases is, you've got to think like a your customer. Don't use key words or key phrases that you think are cool or unique, use key words that a stranger might use to find information on a product or service that you offer. Like on the perfume pages example in **Secret #3,** don't use key phrases like " SYLVIA'S PERFUMES "PERFUME BUSINESS" "PERFUME FRAGRANCES" WOMEN'S PER-FUME "—Use key words that people looking for inf. about dolls would use. Like **"FREEZIA " "COLLECTABLE PERFUMES"** **"BATH & BODY"** etc. Remember also to use the key words and key phrases that are most relevant to your site.

SECRET #5—THE MORE THE MERRIER:

Search engines use spiders (or robots) that search other engines databases as well as the web, for data it may not have in its own files, so the most unusual search engine may provide important information to a more popular engine about your site.

There are so many others using so many search engines, the numbers are staggering. I am convinced that the majority use the top 8. The whole idea of submitting your Website is to get your Website in front of as many people as possible, so the more search engines you submit to, the better off you are.

Another thing to remember is, a lot of the more popular search engines (like Yahoo) can take-up to 6 weeks to index your site, so if you only submit to Yahoo, it will be 6 weeks before any-one can find it. However a lot of engines will index your site automatically (like Infoseek) within seconds, and now the major search engines can find your site with their spiders. Submit your Website to as many searches engines as possible one at a time. It can be a little tedious but it's well worth the effort.

FINAL SECRETS- THINGS NOT TO DO

Using words in your listing like **"HOME PAGE" "WEB SITE"** or **"INTERNET". "SEX"** It's a waste of the limited space you have to describe your site.

USE OF AN UNUSUAL OR CONFUSING WEBSITE NAME.

Your Website title should honestly describe your site and what others can expect to find there. If they don't understand it they won't click on it. List in an inappropriate category. Most people don't use categories to find Websites anyway and listing in categories that aren't relative to your site could cause your Website to be rejected altogether.

Submit your listing before your page is up. Your submission will probably be rejected and just take that much longer. This was discussed in an earlier chapter but I thought it important to say again.

I know this is a lot to absorb, but Search Engine Listings are one OF MY TOP 7 MOST IMPORTANT steps in any online business.

Whether you submit your Website yourself or have a submission service like **Register-it** *http://www.register-it.com* or **Submit-it** *http://www.submit-it.com* does it for you, **DO IT NOW!!!** Every day you wait more of your competitors are getting ahead of you. That's just the way this Internet thing works.

There are companies that can list your site with up to 400 or 500 of the hottest Search Engines in just minutes and are cheap! But when you do it yourself and you do it with the top 8 search engines. You know that your Website **WILL** is registered. You should register your Website the first of each month, as that's when most search engines update their listings. **DO NOT** list your Website more than once. Certain search engines will reject both submissions, **So do not submit it twice or three times** thinking you will get the upper hand on your competitors .Now here are a list of the top 8 search engines and the URL's you will need to go to for your Website registration.

YAHOO: *http://www.yahoo.com/.* To register your Webpage or Website with yahoo you must first go to the category page that bests suites your web site. After you find that you can add your URL by clicking on the icon at the top of the page.
INFOSEEK: *http://www.infoseek.com*
EXCITE: *http://www.excite.com*
ALTA VISTA: *http://www.altavista.com*
LYCOS: *http://www.lycos.com*
HOTBOT: *http://www.hotbot.com*
NORTHERN LIGHT: *http://www.northernlight.com*
WEBCRAWLER: *http://www.webcrawler.com*

These are the search engines that set the standards and rules for the search engine placement game. The problem is that they all have different rules.

So where is the rulebook? There are a couple of different places to obtain the so-called rulebook. You can go to each of the search engines separately and request this information. Visit a couple of the sites that monitor these search engines. Before I mention these sites let me say that in the three years I have been involved with the Internet, the search engines have changed the rules more than once. Why do they do this? I believe it is to try and make the playing field level for everyone. This is so small businesses have the chance to compete with the larger businesses. To keep up with all these rules yourself would take up a tremendous amount of your time. The companies that I am about to mention have done their homework and are excellent sources of information on search engines.

Search Engine Watch *http://www.searchenginewatch.com* / is a great source of information for all the search engines in existence, large and small, new and old. They go into some detail about each search engine and cover a wide variety of topics, absolutely an excellent site. Here is a list of some of the topics they cover:

Webmasters Guide To Search Engines

How search engines index your web site; tips on gaining and maintaining a high position. Make the top ten

Search Engines Facts and Fun

Overview of the major search engines; information on specialty search services; trivia and interesting facts.

Search Engine Status

How search engines are doing, ranging from the financial, to the technical. See the Search Engine EKGs!

Search Engine Resources

`Search engine reviews, tutorials on how to use search engines, insight into search engine technology and more. Search Engine Report and Newsletter Sign-up for this free, monthly update of search engine news; read the current issues or articles from past issues

But the company that covers the top 8 search engines (remember, 85% of the people use only the 8 search engines) and are heads above everyone else is **Planet Ocean Communications**. *http://www.searchenginehelp.com/wave5marketing/*

Planet Ocean puts out a monthly newsletter that critiques those top 8 search engines. Their newsletter is chock full of information that will get you top placement in those search engines. How do I know this works? About two years ago when I was involved with a couple network marketing companies; I had just subscribed to the newsletter. I had only a year's experience on the Internet and building Websites. I was somewhat of a novice, but I didn't let that stop me. I made a dummy network marketing page, used Planet Oceans advice on how to get top placement on Infoseek. I submitted the page, and out of 1,200,000 Websites mine was rated 6th from the top, so what Planet Ocean teaches people really does work.

The cost per year is $197.00 and you are sent an update monthly. This probably the best $197.00 you will ever spend. A high placement in even just one of the top 8 search engines will get you hundreds to thousands of visits. If you have a good product the newsletter will pay for it self; it took me only 2 weeks to see some good results. My suggestion to you is go and visit the site check out their Website and sign up for the search engine news.

Search Engine Forums: *http://searchengineforums.com/bin/*

Ultimate.cgi is a Website that offers different discussion groups for the various search engines. If you have a question about a certain search engine this is the place to go. Discussions are run through out the day, and the times of these different discussions are listed right next to the search engine or topic of which they are associated with.

By doing the things I have listed above will dramatically increase your Website traffic and sales. How many of your competitors are doing these? I'd venture to say that less than 15% of most businesses are using these types of techniques to enhance their Website placement. So by taking a few minutes extra you can go ahead of 85% of the businesses that are your competitors.

Position Agent

Monitor your Web site ranking on the top search engines for many different keywords, and receive weekly e-mail reports. **NEW FEATURES**—Includes Free Web page analyzer to help you improve your Web site listing. **PositionAgent** will test your URL for: search engine readiness, browser compatibility, bad links, and more! Check it out at *http://www.positionagent.com/*

Here is a list of what they do:

1. Monitors Web site rankings using your keywords and URL's;
2. Covers 10 most important search engines and directories;
3. Provides weekly e-mail reports detailing your page and position ranking within the 10 search engines for each URL/keyword combination you choose;
4. Includes integrated Web page analyzer;
5. Reports on all ranked URL's and sub-URL's found for each keyword;
6. Reports on all sites which link to the selected URL (AltaVista only);
7. Provides a Web presence score which you can use to measure the effectiveness of your listings over time;
8. Provides graphic reports for each URL/keyword combination that you can access at any time at the PositionAgent Web site;
9. Lets you change your URL/keyword selections at any time;
10. Allows access to the service for six months.

Here is another Website that will help you with your Website placement:

http://www.magic-city.net/

Magic City will get your site listed in the top 20 of the major search engines.

If you did not create your own site, talk to your Webmaster and ask she/he about the things I have listed. Be sure to check out my Website *http://www.wave5marketing.com* for an in-depth book on all the tricks of the top 8 search engines.

Chapter 15

Keywords!
What are they And How Do They Work?

"Imagination is more important than knowledge."

—Albert Einstein

When I think of keywords, I think of Website submission. Keywords are what people use when they are doing a search for a particular subject using a search engine. When making a Website and viewing it through a web browser like Internet Explorer 4.0 or Netscape Navigator 4.0 go to the tool bar on top of the web browser and click on the view button. After you have clicked on the view button a menu appears. Go to the word "source and click on it. You will now see how a Web page looks in "HTML (hypertext markup language). If you scroll down you will see a line that looks like this:

<META NAME="keywords" CONTENT="localization, Chinese, China, hi-tech, business, international, bilingual, joint venture, cooperation, import, export, consulting, Asia, language, translation, ChinaNet, finance, promotion"> After the word content are the keywords. When you make a Website and submit it to the search engines of your choice, they index your page based upon what you entered for keywords. The way a lot of these search engines index your Website, is they send out a scanbot (this is like an automated robot) to scan your Website.

The scanbot scans your Website for various items and keywords is one of the items it scans for. When it scans your keywords the scanbot will take this information back to the search engine and have those keywords filed in a database.

Just as an example lets say you had a bakery business and you wanted to sell your bakery products over the Internet. You have a prospective customer that uses his web browser to locate one of the top 8 major search engines. He then uses the search engine to locate businesses like yours. When the prospect gets to the search engine of their choice they type a keyword into the search box. In this case you would type in either bakery, or bakery products for your keywords. You could also type in keywords like pies, or cakes. After you do this you click on the search button and the search engine will then list, usually in groups of 10, Website that have been indexed with the keywords you have done your search for.

Banner Ad Keywords

Key words are also used in banner ads. Depending on what you sell, having the best keywords in that particular subject is a definite advantage whether you are using them for a banner ad or your

Website. If you want to find those keywords that are most often used go to The Word Spot Website at *http://www.wordspot.com/custom.html*.

You can also use the search engines and type what you think may be the best keyword for the subject you are searching for. Then check out the top 10 Websites for the keyword entered. When the Websites come into view, check out the source page and the keywords that they used. This may be a good reason why their Websites are in the top 10.

There are millions of keywords used everyday, so how do you know which ones are best? Don't just guess what keywords to use when setting up your Web pages to index to the search engines. Get up to date information at Word Spot. If you go to their Website and tell them what your five primary keywords are, you will receive weekly, a report that has all of the keywords that are used most often used with the keywords you supplied them.

With this report you will know how people misspell your keywords, discover new keywords that you would never have thought of. By doing this you will have found another opportunity to increase traffic to your Website. The words that Word Spot gives you were statistically sampled in searches done on the "World Wide Web". The sampling is performed on several search engines every 3 to 5 minutes every day over 20 hours, 7 days a week.

If you are looking to start up a new business or write reports or articles that you can sell over the Internet on a on a popular subject, then Word spot is the place to go.

How To Use Misspellings To Give You That Competitive Edge

Earlier I talked of misspellings. When deciding on your keywords, misspelled words are a good thing to include in your keyword selection. You will be surprised how often words are misspelled. This is one way to put you one up on your competitors, so include the misspelled words as part of your keyword arsenal. Here is a great site for misspelled words: *http://www.spellweb.com/* SpellWeb is an evolving experiment in "sidesifting" the Web for useful patterns of information. If you enter two misspellings of a word, it will show you, the one more popular, though neither one, is right. You can either include one or both under your Meta keyword tags. SpellWeb can also be used to judge relative popularity based on occurrence on the Web. Check out your favorite Network Marketing Company Usana vs. Market America or Football vs. Basketball. If are trying to decide on what business to enter into on the Internet, SpellWeb can give you the edge.

Chapter 16

Places To Advertise Online and How to Advertise

"A teacher affects eternity, he can never tell, where his influence stops."

—Henry B. Adams

Stay Organized

Before you start on your classified ad campaign you need to be organized and have an advertising schedule. What you need is set up a spreadsheet and keep track of which company submitted your ad to and what day. The best way is set up your ads on a 2-week rotation. By doing this you will keep your ad close to the top of the list. Don't let it run over the 2 weeks. If you do your ad will sift towards the bottom and possibly off of the list all together. If possible get an e-mail address or phone number of the company running the classified ad. Call them up and ask them what day they post new ads and what time of day they post them. Usually the last ads that are posted are listed at the top. Sometimes this is done right after midnight.

Your Schedule

Pick out three days of the week to submit your ad. The three best days are usually Monday, Wednesday, and Friday. Submit 5 separate ads on each of these days. Remember the spreadsheet that I set up for each of the classifieds. Let's put that spreadsheet to some use now. Leave a category on the spreadsheet for a tracking code. I use a name or numbering system. In all my ads I offer a FREE report.

Here is an example of the headlines I use: *"Discover how you can attract thousands of prospects to your Website."* To receive a free report in seconds by Autoresponder, e-mail me: *bbrolhorst@wave5market-ing.com* my tracking word is *"classifieds"*. When I check my Autoresponder for e-mail addresses I look for my keywords. This will tell me what ads drew the most responses. Then I know what interests my prospects are looking for. I enter this information into my spreadsheet and keep the results for a year. Now I have important information to decide if I want to continue with the headline I was using or try a different one.

There are over 10,000 classifieds on the Internet that you can advertise for FREE. By posting to 15 classifieds per week that would be a total of 30 ads in your 2-week cycle. In time, you will have a powerhouse of classifieds that you can refer back to time after time, and all this for FREE. Listed below are a couple of sites that you can go to find a utility that will enable you to send out multiple classifieds all at the same time.

http://www.tunza-products.com/classified/ads_7.html

How to use each site, without having to retype your ad, over and over again. All you do is "click", and then place your ad. IT'S THAT EASY! "The Classified Ad Broadcaster " will now let you enter your ad once, and have it broadcasted to hundreds of other web sites—INSTANTLY! All you have to do is become a member the membership fee is $29.95 to order paste this URL into your web browser. *http://www.tunza-products.com/classified/order.html*

I ran across a software program that will automate submission of your classified ads. With this submission wizard you will have access to over 1300 classified sites. You can submit your classified ad to 300 free sites within minutes. If you would submit these manually it could take you days or even weeks. The name of the software is Classify 98; you can either download this program in a temporary file on your hard drive or try it out to a limited number of sites Free. Or you can download the full version. Check it out at the Trellian site at *http://www.trellian.com/classify/index*

If you choose to use the submission software or if you decide you would like to send them out manually you will still need some free sites to advertise at. Here are a couple of sites that list free sites to advertise in:
http://www.mlm-exchange.com/directory/classifieds1.htm

Listed in the site below are 250 free and low cost classifieds that can generate 1000's of hits per day.
http://www.mlm-exchange.com/directory/classifieds1.htm

Called the granddaddy of free classifieds where you will find over 3000 free classifieds. *http://www.ecki.com/links/index.shtml#index http://ecki.com/links/7class.shtml* Check out both of these sites.

Commerce Corner offers over 20,000 sites that the world will see. Just submit 1 ad and they take care of the rest. Commerce Corner also offers Image Ads, and Banner Advertising for a very small fee. Check out their rates at: *http://www.comcorner.com/costs.html*

These sites will keep you busy submitting your ads and keeping up with all the response you will receive. Be prepared to make some serious cash.

Be Persistent and Consistent

Don't procrastinate! This can be a very powerful marketing tool. Your have to take the time to set it up correctly and be willing to do everything just as I mentioned above. Set up a schedule of things to do everyday. When the task is complete check it off and move on to the next task.

Test Test Test

O.K. you have made it this far the rest is easy. You have run through 4 cycles that is 2 months of submitting ads. You see that some of the ads are just not pulling in many responses. Don't waste your time submitting to them, drop them and move on to a new classified. This can be somewhat time consuming but if you are persistent you will end up with many responses. Another way to get to your target market is to advertise in e-zines. What E-zines should you advertise in? Go to *http://www.lifestylespub.com/cgi-bin/ezines.cgi?10002*

Opt-In mail lists for categories of newsletters pertaining to what type of products or services that you want to target: *http://www.targ-it.com/lists.htm*

Running an ad in an e-zine is one of the quickest ways to get your classified out to thousands. By advertising in classifieds you could submit it on Wednesday have it published by Friday and by Friday evening you could already be getting response to your ad. When advertising in an e-zine you should subscribe to the e-zine (also known as newsletters) become familiar and read the archives if they offer one.

Read some of the classifieds that were submitted. If you see the same ad posted many times then you know that whoever posted the ad is getting some good responses or you would not continue to see the ad. This can also be a good way to see how to write an ad. Look for ads that sell similar products or services. Adjust the ad to fit your ad and offer a FREE report. This is a sure-fire way to get a response.

The Classified Club
http://www.hitekhosting.net/cgi-bin/club_click.cgi?ID75 was developed to assist both the new and the veteran Internet marketer. The club is packed with the newest in classified ad resources, tools, tips, and know-how to get you the traffic and orders you need…now!

Chapter 17

Get Your Name On The
Bill Boards of the Internet

"Although our inattention can contribute to our lack of total well-being,
we also have the power to choose positive behaviors and responses.
In that choice we change our every experience in life."

—Greg Anderson

Banner ads seem to becoming less and less popular. Why is that? Well to begin with banner ads seemed to be more of a fad that everyone was doing a couple of years ago. By looking at some of the few hundred Websites that I visit in a week's time it has become apparent that this is true. So should we give up on banner ads completely, I don't think so.

The search engines still seem to be using them in full force, and if they are using them then we need to take a closer look. Banner ads on a search engine work differently then they would on your own Website. The difference between the two is that when you place a banner ad on a search engine they don't care if someone clicks on it and leaves. They know that you will be back to search another time.

As far as your own Website is concerned you have tried hard to attract prospects to your site. Do you really want to sell banner advertising on your site and take the risk of losing a prospect? I still think you can have your cake and eat it to. If you set up your site correctly you can have a few banner ads placed on your first pages that will make you some good money. Towards the end of your site you could have a full page of banner ads.

What I have done is developed banner ads for local area merchants. Since they already have an advertising budget they were more than willing to pay for banner ads on my Website. The cost to them was about a third of what they would pay in local area newspapers and other publications.

Another item of consideration is if you run a highly trafficked Website and are high in the search engine listings (you need to be able to have proof of this). You will be able to charge more for your banner ad space because of the increased exposure you will get.

A New Twist To an Old Idea

If you have been connected to Internet for a very long time, or if you are new to the Internet you probably have received some e-mail at one time or another that had 5 names and addresses in the subject. If out of those 5 names you send $5.00 to each name. You then take off the first name listed and place your name and address to the bottom of the list. After so much time you will receive X amount of money. Well this turned out to be a scam, because you had no way of knowing if the people that were involved would do the same thing.

With banner ads and you could use the same idea and the best part about it is, it cost you nothing but your time, unless you had a Webmaster building your site. Any way here is how it could be set up and what you could expect. The way it works is very simple which is why it could produce some enormous results. This is free and open to all sites profit or not.

By displaying a total of 5 banners on your web site, in a few months time you could have your banner ad exposed in a minimum of 600 web sites. Here's how it would work, suppose only 5 (This number could be much larger especially if your the Webmaster of a free links page so let's keep this example simple) Webmasters visit your site and join banner explode. Let's also suppose each of those 5 web sites are also visited by 5 Webmasters who join and the cycle continues until your banner cycles through fourth position. The Result is 5x5x5x5=625. Your Banner is displayed at 625 sites! I haven't tried this yet, but when I have the time to set it up, I think it will be fun to see how it works and what kind of response I get. The best part about it is that it is **Free**.

Good banner ads don't provide a lot of information about the site or service. That is the job of the site itself. The banner should grab their attention. It should scream 'I know something you don't, but I will tell you." Don't overlook humor. It is the best way to get click-through.

Link Exchange *http://adnetwork.linkexchange.com/*

Link exchange offers free banner ads for all of its members. Simply put, you display banners for members of the network, and they in turn display banners for you. A portion of the banner space is sold to sponsors, through whose support the network stays free. They also have a discussion group (newsgroups) for the discussion of things banner, which is one of the more active discussion groups about new advertising. You should subscribe even if you don't join the banner exchange. Has over 50,000 advertising members and serves up over 3 million banners every day.

http://www.markwelch.com/bannerad/

An extensive site that reviews many of the players in the banner agency field. Has a strong focus on agencies that promise a lot and deliver not at all. Follow this site when buying or selling.

http://www.melizo.com/area52/search2/macinsearch/banners/

Banner swap clubs just for Macintosh sites. Rumors of the Mac's death are greatly exaggerated.

e/y/e/s/c/r/e/a/m/ interactive inc. *http://www.exposure-usa.com/*

This is one of the leading on-line agencies around. They do killer creative and negotiate excellent media buys for their clients. There is a lot of information on their web site that will help you learn more about on-line advertising and creative. Drop by and look around. If you have on-line media for sale, make sure you are in their database.

An extensive site that reviews many of the players in the banner agency field. Has a strong focus on agencies that promise a lot and deliver not at all. Follow this site when buying or selling. New Gate Internet Inc. *http://www.newgate.net/.* Companies who place banner advertising often use their money inefficiently. It is common practice for businesses to place ads on any number of the top 40 most busy web sites, such as Yahoo or Netscape in hopes that, by sheer volume of impressions, the traffic to their site will increase. To help you use your advertising budget more efficiently, NewGate will pinpoint more targeted and thus more effective web sites to maximize your banner buys. There are thousands of sites on the Net that have more focused demographics than the top-40 traffic sites, but are often overlooked. NewGate specializes in finding this audience for you.

Making Your Own Banner Ad Free

The Banner Generator *http://www.coder.com/creations/banner/*

The Banner Generator is a free service to let you create graphical banners for your web pages. If you get stuck, please check the Frequently Asked Questions and the Instructions. You can use The Banner Generator to create title banners for web pages, hyperlinked buttons, or banner ads. Simply fill out and submit *The Banner Generator Form.* After you submit the form, it will take about five to ten seconds for your banner to be generated. You will see a page called "Banner Created." It will tell you the URL of your banner on our server.

http://www.mediabuilder.com/abm.html

Create your own custom animated banners at this Website. No fancy plug-ins or hard thinking required. Choose any one of the animation effects at the Media Builder Website. Type the text you want to appear on your banner. Click the "Make Banner" button. After the banner is created, you can save the banner to your own computer

6 Steps To Increase Click Through On Your Banner Ads

There are many ways to improve click rates. Here are a few that have been proven to help:

Step # 1) Place banner at the top of the page, or top and bottom.
Step # 2) Don't group the banner with other advertisements.
Step # 3) Place the banner code on several pages and on your busiest pages.
Step # 4) Put banners at points where visitors usually exit your site.
Step # 5) Use a unique border that will stand out and attract attention.
Step # 6) Use a large type or font, with fewer words.

Use a gray or yellow background, both these work exceptionally well, but gray out performs the yellow background. Other colors that work well are Orange, Blue, and Green. **"Click Here"** has stood the test of time and seems to entice viewers to do just as you ask. The number one drawing card in banner advertising is the use of the word **FREE**. Write a report that solves a problem and post it at your Website. Offer a free drawing, or a free subscription to a newsletter. Free advertising or free software works great to. Never assume that your viewer knows what to do next. Always, in one or more places insert the words "Click Here" or Click Here Now! Or use a drop down menu with a click arrow displayed prominently.

A warning banner is an enormously powerful approach. Terms like **"Warning! Before you purchase Vitamins"**, Click here first" or " **Warning! Click here before you Advertise"**

Do not use company logos! People are really not interested in your company name; they are more interested in a benefit that you can provide for them. This is true on your Website as well.

Test, test, and test some more. Never assume that you have made the perfect banner ad. If you are designing your own banner ad, or some other company is doing it for you, you should be running at least 3 or 4 banner ads at the same time to see which ones are getting the best response. To get the statistics on the information for visits to your web page, contact your web hosting company. Most good ones will track this information for you at no extra cost to you. Just ask! Review your stats daily and when you see a banner starting to lag be prepared to act quickly.

Remember the three most important elements of your banner ad. First your copy, next the color, and finally your graphics. Mix and match these three elements until you see what combination works the best for you. One thing that concerns Website owners when placing banner ads is that when people click on them they leave their site. Even the viewers don't like the idea of leaving, especially if they like what you offer at your site.

There are a couple solutions to this problem. The first is to design your banner ad to say, **"Click here for free inf. and never leave this site"**. These are known as Host Friendly banner ads. When they click on your ad, a message or free report is sent automatically to their mailbox by use of an Auto-Responder. (Check out the Auto-Responder chapter) You do this by leaving a hard copy link to your Auto-Responder. The second solution is to place above or below the banner ad a line that says, " Please bookmark this page before you click on the banner.

If you would like to learn more about banner ads, a good source of information is Mark Welchs' discussion group on banner ads. Check out Marks Website at *http://www.egroups.com/list/wsba-digest/*. This discussion group is free so take advantage, learn, and have fun doing it.

I am a big supporter of non-picture banner ads because it reduces in load up time of a Website. For an idea of some of the

best non-picture banner ads that can work for you check out some of the top rated ones at:
http://www.whitepalm.com/fourcorners/bestctrnonpic.shtml

Remember that just like the other marketing efforts described in this course not one of them were designed primarily has a single source of income. They are supposed to be used in conjunction with each other to gain you maximum exposure and earn you top dollar for your efforts.

By far the most highly recommended program is WebAdverts, which I went ahead and installed on my site. It's easy enough to setup and works just great.

It is a shareware program that costs $50 to register if you decide to keep it. You can download it from *http://awsd.com/scripts/webadverts*

http://www.e-ads.net/
Check this out before you print it
http://sellitontheweb.com/ezine/product008.shtml%20.

Chapter 18

Malls

"Ideas without action are worthless."

—Harvey Mackay

Using a Cybermall

If you're creating a business in the real world, a shopping mall is a great place to be. The problem is, it's expensive. But on the Internet, there are lots of cybermalls, and they've all got afford-able accounts. You can have your Web site hosted by a cybermall, and be alongside all those other businesses! Think of the traffic! Well, whoop-de-do. Don't believe the cybermall hype. Generally speaking, cybermalls are a lousy deal. In cyberspace, they're pointless. Businesses don't need to be grouped together. You don't need parking in cyberspace, you don't need a food hall, and if you want to watch a movie after shopping you'll leave your computer. Cybermall accounts are usually more expensive than a good Web hosting account, and provide very few benefits. And in some cases they provide really atrocious Web-creation skills (my favorite quote: "As a bartender I made minimum wage plus tips; as an Internet Consultant I now make $100 an hour." Do you really want a bartender designing your Web site?)

At least one cybermall runs "Get Rich on the Internet" seminars around the U.S., encouraging people to become cybermall "consultants," selling space and Web design services to any and all. Stay away from cybermalls, they're not worth the trouble.

Chapter 19

Bulk E-Mail & Opt-in E-mail

"Nurture your mind with great thoughts,
for you will never go any higher than you think."

—Benjamin Disraeli

Does bulk e-mail work? Well there are some people that use bulk e-mail and claim that it works well for them. But by using bulk e-mail you stand the chance of making a certain amount of your recipients angry because of the fact that they did not request the information you have sent them. There is a word for bulk e-mail and it is known as spam mail. There are many things that can happen when spamming or let's call it bulk e-mail is sent out. Many of the things that can happen are more bad than there are good.

The good things that come out of bulk e-mail is that you are reaching a high volume of people. Some bulk e-mail lists reach into the millions of people that will see your ad and are relatively low in cost. Not too many good reasons to bulk e-mail are there.

Now the bad side, by using bulk e-mail you stand a very good chance of getting booted off of your Internet Service Provider or your Web hosting company. Why? Because of the complaints that they can receive from the people you sent the bulk e-mail. This is not a fairy tale, as many of the bulk e-mail companies want you to believe it is. It is happening and happening with more and more frequency. People that bulk e-mail usually have to switch from one ISP to another. Certain Internet Service Providers allow you to send and receive only so many pieces of mail; this is especially true with America Online. So a word to the wise is check with your ISP and see what there guidelines for bulk e mailing are before you do it.

Another area of concern is replies known as "flames". The definition of getting flamed is getting e-mail from people that you have sent bulk e-mail to. What some people will do is send you a nasty e-mail telling you of their discontent. A flame can also be someone sending you hundreds of the same e-mail. This clutters up your e-mail mailbox. You then have to take the time to delete these nasty e-mails (more time wasted).

It takes up bandwidth which with the amount of new people getting on the Internet daily is shrinking. Bandwidth is the ability to send X amount of information whether it is e-mail or downloading a Website into your browser. If your bulk e-mail reaches people in countries outside of the United States you are costing these people even more money. How is this so? Most foreign countries do not have the telephone systems like we have in the states. These people outside the U.S. are paying for every minute they are online and the rates are much higher. Mix into the fact that most of bulk e-mail goes out to people that have no interests in your products or services.

Finally the last reason that I would never bulk e-mail is in don't know how good these lists are or whether they even send out the amount of e-mail that they said they do. How many of these bulk e-mail addresses are current? How many times has that list been used by others? Just a couple of days ago I received some e-mail from a company that distributes bulk email. They said that my ad would be sent out to 62 million people. From the last survey I saw the number was up to 150 million people worldwide as of November 1998, that is over more than a third of the people online. Although this could be true I still find it very hard to believe.

If you absolutely insist on bulk e mailing then I suggest you do a couple of things. First you should get a free e-mail account. Check out these sites as to which ones will let you send and receive unlimited e-mail.

Places To Get Free E-mail Accounts

Bigfoot: *http://www.bigfoot.com*
Net Address: *http://www.usa.net*
Vlaise: *http://www.valise.com*
Hotmail: *http://www.hotmail.com*
Pronto Mail: *http://www.commtouch.com*
Juno: *http://www.juno.com*

I

If you need a free ISP then look no farther you can have it at Freeweb. Check out heir Website at:
http://www.freewwweb-access.com/freeweb.cgi?id=1034-12

The second thing you should do is set up an e-mail filtering system.

That can filter out flames or eliminate any unwanted e-mail by typing in keywords that are in headlines of incoming mail.
Filtering Systems

Pegasus *http://www.pegasus.usa.com/*
Eudora at *http://eudora.qualcomm.com/products/*
   Both are free software programs that I have found works the best for filtering, but I can't comment on bulk e-mail because I have never used it.

   Eudora makes an upgraded version of its filtering software known as Eudora Pro. This software is not free, but the cost is minimal and its features are a lot better than Eudora. There are differences between Eudora Pro and Pegasus. If You are interested than go look at all three of the filtering systems. I think you need to see all three and then decide which one works best for you.

   I also suggest that you set up a couple of different databases. One for your happy customers, these you want to stay in touch with. The other for those customers that you have gotten negative mail from that you don't want to include on your future mailing lists. Not only should you have the things listed above for bulk e-mail but for opt in lists as well.

   Another way of sending out large amounts of mail is by using a dedicated "List Serv" What is a dedicated List Serv? It is software for running your own Internet email mailing lists, such as discussions, announcement lists, newsletters, and auto-responders. It's easy, fast and powerful! What can you all do with a List Serv? You can have your mail server reject spam, prevent unauthorized mail relaying and halt email bombs! Here are some of the companies that offer this type of software:

http://www.lyris.com/lyris.html
http://www.mailshield.com/
http://www.talklist.com/
http://www.lsoft.com/lists/listref.html

Opt-In Mail Lists

Enough about bulk e-mail. Let me introduce to e-mail lists that work the best for the people that send out their sales pitches and for the people that are receiving them. Here are some stats that compare various types of mail lists based on click through.

Bulk (spam) email—0.1%
Banner ads—1-3%
Direct (snail) mail—1-5%
Opt-In email lists—5-7%

An opt-in list is made up of people that at one time or another have requested the products or services that you sell. How do they do this? By filling out surveys or forms requesting information in various categories such as computers, home study courses, cars, food, or just about any subject you can think of. In these forms and surveys the people that are conducting them, ask for contact information. The reason for this, when new products or services become available the people that have filled out these forms and surveys are then contacted if they have shown an interest in receiving them. These list are then sold to companies that want to target prospective buyers of their products or services. Your return on investment is much higher than if you used bulk e-mail even though these lists are more expensive.

Opt-in lists are an extremely effective alternative to spam. Opt-in lists are lists of prospects that voluntarily subscribed, or "opted" into the list. They are not on the list against their will—they want to be on the list and receive relevant information and offers. Also, opt-in list members are free to remove their name from the list at any time. There is no obligation. Not only can some buy an Opt-In List to find prospects for their business, but if you are looking to buy products or services you can be added to a Opt-In list and be contacted by companies selling the products or services that you have showed an interest in.

Just as an example and don't hold me to these figures, I want you to get an idea of how these different lists compare. Let's say that you buy a list of bulk e-mail, of 50,000 e-mail addresses. Out of the list you get 1 out of every 100 of people to respond. That would be 500 responses. Out of those 500 you get 1% or 5 people to buy your product or service.

5 Steps when looking For A Opt-In List

Step # 1

Use a reputable service. Ask for referrals. I don't know of any scams, But I expect that, as the popularity of opt-in grows, the number of impostors will, too. Most services ask for cash up front, so be sure that you know whom you're dealing with.

Step # 2

Distinguish between list owners (e.g. Webpromote) and list brokers (e.g. PostMaster Direct). Make sure that a broker, who contracts out to use several lists, is not mailing to the same list you used last week!

Step # 3

Use lists that appeal to your audience, and avoid generalized ones if you can. Some companies, like PostMaster Direct, have very specific lists.

Step # 4

Keep track of your visitors via a special page or a closed loop to see what they do. Lists can be reused, and you can learn something about a particular list that may be useful if you mail to the same group later.

Step # 5

Don't give up on other forms of web advertising just because opt-in e-mail works. The bulk of opt-in responses occur within 24 hours of the mailing, so then what do you have running? The number of opt-in companies with good lists are still small, and the resource is limited.

Sample Price List
Number of Addresses and Price Per Address
1,500—2,999 10 cents
3,000—4,999 8 cents
5,000—9,999 6.5 cents
10,000 + 5 cents

Sample Opt-In Mail

Below is an example of how your advertisement will be seen in your prospects e-mail box.

Return-Path: <postmaster@opt-inlist.com>
To: johndoe@hisaddress.com
From: xxxsupport <mail@opt-inlist.com>
Date: Mon., 16 Nov 1998 20:02:17
Subject: Opt-In Mail Lists!
-=-

This is a Wave 5 Marketing Targeted e-MailOpt-Inlist. To Subscribe To Select Targeted Lists to Mail To: http://www.opt-inlists.com List Removal Instructions are at the end of this message.
-=-
John Doe:

We are proud to announce the launch of the latest version of our Internet Opt-In list Solution—Opt-In lists. Did you know your customers could write you for an opt-in mail list online? As a Web Merchant, using our Mail List Commerce Software, your customers can order your mail lists right at your Website! http://www.maillist.com Visit us today, and look at all the great new Features we've included. You can even download our Trialware and print your mail lists directly from our Website.
Best Regards,

Mail List Commerce
Product Support
[Mail List Targeted Service]
johndoe@hisaddress.com
Mail List Database Removal Instructions:

To easily be removed from future Mail Lists, go to the following URL and enter any e-mail addresses that you would like to have removed.
http://www.maillist.com/be_removed.htm

By trusting the opt-in list company you deal with (there are many good companies which are listed below) you will always have a place you can go to and get responsive leads.

http://www.inboxexpress.com/targeted_lists.htm
http://www.netextensions1.com/cgi/members/AD98.html

http://www.postmasterdirect.com/
http://www.motivatedseller.com/wgreorde.html

The best Opt-In list found on the Internet is the one that you have made up from your own surveys and sales. Here is how to develop an Opt-In list of your own. From your Website you create a form with questions for your visitors to answer. In this form you ask such as

#1 Were there products or services that I don't have on my Website that you are interested in?
#2 Are there articles on information that you would be interested in seeing?
#3 What types of software would you use to operate your business online?

These are just a few sample questions that could increase your sales and get return visits of your customers or future prospects. Always ask for your customers contact information. When forming your own Opt-In mail list make sure that your prospects know that their name will not be sold, traded or given away. You will get a much higher response rate if you let your prospects know that their contact information is safe. Another way to build you own Opt-In mailing list is to offer them a free newsletter.

Chapter 20

How To Use Chatrooms
To Promote Your Business

"Be grateful for luck, but don't depend on it."

—William Feather

What are some of the subjects that people on the Internet like to chat about? Business, computers, sports, entertainment, health, and a range of other topics. Many chat rooms are entirely social, intended for anyone who simply wants to correspond with others. You can even join special chat events featuring celebrities or other important figures.

Chat is a fast-paced form of Internet discussion. When you chat on the Internet, you "talk" to others by typing them messages on your keyboard. Although there are thousands of different types of Internet chat, they all follow the same basic rules. To join a chat, you enter a "chat room" where people gather. Part of your screen shows the nicknames of the other people in the room. Another segment shows the text of the "conversation" the chatters are engaged in. You can join any time by typing your own remarks, which the other chatters will see immediately.

AOL Chatrooms

My favorite place to go for Chatrooms is AOL. I appreciate the way AOL has setup the lists of different Chatrooms. They are easy to navigate from one Chatrooms to the next, and they offer a wide variety.

Chatroom Etiquette

Rule #1) Lurk before you leap

Before you join in on the conversations in a Chatroom get a feel for what the discussion is about. A good way to see if the Chatroom interests you.

Rule #2) Politeness

If you are pleasant and helpful in any Chatroom you will be respected. By being respected people will seek you out for the information that they know you possess.

Rule # 3 Respect others opinions and businesses

Remember that your business is not the only business in these Chatrooms. Other peoples business is very important to them. Just like a customer if you put their needs first, your business will flourish.

Rule # 4 Be active

Don't sit back and just listen, become an active member of any Chatroom that you frequent. You'll surprise yourself how many new friends and business acquaintances you will make when you participate in these Chatrooms.

Rule #5 Promoting your business

If you frequent any Chatroom be sure to fill out a profile. Your profile should be exactly like your SIG file for your e-mail account. Everyone that fills out a profile will be asked to enter a screen name. This can be anything you want it to be. Most people try to have their screen name reflect their business. Remember with most of these Chatrooms when you are choosing your screen name that they limit you to around 11 characters. Mine on AOL is **wave5mktng**. People can check out what your business is by reading your profile. I can't count the number of times that I have received e-mail from someone that was in a Chatroom when I was there, even though I never had any communication with them.

Rule # 6) Free reports

Marketing through Chatrooms is really no different than marketing through discussion groups, or by using a classified ad. People in these Chatrooms can be skeptical at times, but if there is a subject that is being discussed and I have information on it, I will jump in and give my opinion. That is when I offer a free report. Talk about breaking the ice, when you offer any thing for FREE people really warm up to you. I have made a ton of sales using this tactic, besides becoming a credible person for the information that you know.

Rule # 7 Bartering

I have made many new business associates bartering my services. What is Barter? Barter is an exchange of products or services with other business people and no money is exchanged. Simply put, you have something someone else wants and they have something you want. Bartering can also be a form of advertising your services or products. Bartering gives you the chance to show case your products or services. I have bartered my services with Webmasters, office organizers, software producers, and even printing companies. By bartering the word of my services and products have not only reached the people that I have bartered with but it has reached their customers as well and people that their customers know and. well you get the point. This can be a very powerful marketing tool and one that I suggest you seriously consider.

Web Based Chat

This is the easiest form of chat and is great for beginners. If you have a web browser that supports Java, like recent versions of Netscape Navigator and Microsoft Internet Explorer, you can often leap right into a Web based chat room and start talking. All the Chatrooms available to you through your Personal Start Page channels feature this type of chat. Some Web based chats request that you have a browser plug in installed.

Internet Relay Chat

Also commonly known as "IRC". The Internet offers some of the same type of Chatrooms that America Online does. IRC Chatrooms is simple to find. All you have to do is go to a search engine like Yahoo, Hot Bot, Infoseek, Excite, or any of the top 8 or 10 search engines. In the subject box type IRC chat and you will have a list of different Chatrooms. Pick the one that interests you the most and click on it and your there.

Check out the Palace they have over 1,000 Chatrooms that you'll have to see to believe, hundreds of which are open at any given time. You can find everything from the Small Business Convention Center to just about any other Chatroom imaginable If you're not sure what you're looking for, take your time and look through The Palace A-Z list at *http://www.thepalace.com/welcome/sites/az.html*

IRC takes place on several networks of special chat servers all over the world. IRC is a bit more challenging for beginners but offers the widest variety of chat rooms. For those of you that are new to IRC I have found a great Website that offers some great advice for the novice. *http://www.newircusers.com/*

Business Chatrooms

http://www.zdnet.com/cc/chat.html

Zdnet is one of the leaders online in marketing experience and their business chat room is a good one. Go to there site and download their Virtual Places software and your ready to chat.

AOL's Entrepreneurs Chatroom
Your Own Chatroom on your Website

One way to make your Web site attractive to visitors is to add a chat room. You can set up "celebrity" chats periodically, and invite people to attend; hold "lectures," have a technical-support chat room, in which your customers can ask questions; or just have an open chat room, in which visitors to your site can chat with others. Chat rooms really can help a Web site's popularity. As Jason Olim, President of Condo, has said, "There are lots of Internet buzzwords, and most are nonsense. The only really valid one is community. If people visit your site to be with other, like-minded, people, then you're on your way to success." A Website chat room can help you create that community, as well as guaranteeing return visits of past visitors or customers.

Here is a list of Websites that can help you with Website Chatrooms
http://beseen.com/chat/mr-index.html

Set up your own Website Chatroom FREE at Beseen.com. Here is what they have to say about their free Chatroom: No downloads, no installs, no HTML or CGI scripts to master, and no waiting for Java; it's easy to use and easy to set-up.
http://homebusinessgroup.com/reseller_info.htm

http://www.talkcity.com/irc/apply.html

In my opinion Talk City has one of the top most comprehensive chat sites on the "WWW". You can get a list of calendar of events of different chats sent right to your mail box all you have to do is enter your e-mail address at:
http://www.talkcity.com/tcp/subscribe.html

Chapter 21

Using Newsletters To Increase Sales Without Spending A Dime

"For they conquer who believe they can."

—Virgil

If there is any particular marketing tool that will boost your sales of your products or services more than anything else, it has to be publishing an online newsletter.

What is an E-mail Newsletter? Newsletters are published by many organizations, from schools to churches to businesses. They can be updates of upcoming events, new products, or just about any topic you can think of to keep readers up to date on what ever business or hobby you are interested in.

So why is it called an e-mail newsletter? It is news that you want to pass onto existing customers or new prospects by e-mail. The newsletters can be delivered daily, weekly, or monthly to your subscribers' desktop. Newsletters are not sent out randomly, they are sent to people that requested them. By sending out newsletters randomly you are bordering on spam. So what is the cost for publishing your newsletter? To publish your newsletter it will cost you nothing other than your time unless you have a subscriber base of more than 200 subscribers.

For a list of under 200 subscribers you can use a FREE software program called Lyris. Check out their website at: http://www.lyris.com/sales.html

If your list is larger than 200 subscribers then you will need to invest in software or a company that can handle sending out a large amount of e-mail newsletters.

If you are a newsletter author then you need to contact go to http://www.listpartners.com/cgi-local/addpartner?143. Their specialty is serving newsletter authors. They offer professional level distribution and list management services, ad sales assistance, fast and friendly customer service, reasonable prices, and even the opportunity to earn a FREE account. By far the best list service on the internet.

Check out their website and see why so many other email authors call it the best service.

Information Overload

Don't go over board on your content. What I like to see is about a 2-page newsletter, something that is informative but not so large as to lose you subscribers' interest. Keep in mind that you are not writing a book, so keep it short. If your newsletter has good content and is well organized your subscribers will appreciate reading it. By keeping it short you will keep your readers interest and your subscriber base will grow. Don't overload them with information. Usually 5 to 6 topics are plenty. Just like a good diet a little bit at a time is easier to digest.

If your newsletter is beneficial to people they will be long time subscribers and the news of your newsletter will bring in many new subscribers. To start out with you should have an outline of the topics you want to cover in each newsletter. For the novice I suggest that the newsletter be sent monthly until you get an idea of the time it will take to publish your newsletter.

Future Newsletters

When I am writing my own newsletter I have ideas pop into my head as I am writing it. What I do instead of making the newsletter to large and overloading my subscribers with information is I jot down these ideas. By doing this I save myself time and I'm assured of having fresh content. Then at the end of the newsletter I tell my subscribers of the upcoming articles that they will read about in future issues. Now you have a head start on your next newsletter. You will surprise yourself at the ideas that you get once you start writing your newsletter.

What I like to do is keep the newsletter reader friendly, much like a piece of e-mail from someone you know. If you are using a word processor to publish the newsletter make sure to use your spell checker to make sure everything is spelled right and looks professional. Remember this is your business that you are trying to promote and by having misspelled words you can lose your credibility.

Web Browsers

If you don't have a word processor you can use a web browser like Netscape Navigator that has a spell checker installed in the software and you can download the latest version of it free by going to this Website. *http://home.netscape.com/computing/download/*

If you do use a word processor like Microsoft Word and you want to use Links to other sites in your newsletter and you want to see how your newsletter will look to your subscribers then you should cut and paste it into your web browser. In Netscape you can check your links to make sure that they aren't broken and that the Website you want your subscribers to link to is still in operation.

Staying Within Your Guidelines

One of my pet peeves is to click on a link and wait for it to download only to find out that the Website no longer exists. I have just wasted my time. If you want to keep your subscribers make sure that the links that you use are not broken. When publishing your newsletter always use headers to separate the different subjects and keep your paragraphs short. Your newsletter will be much easier to read and it won't fatigue your readers. Don't go outside of what your computer screen can give you. To me it is irritating to have to scroll from side to side as well as up and down. If I have to scroll from side to side I lose my interest and sometimes I lose track of where I am at in the newsletter. So keep it simple and within your computer screen. A good rule of thumb is to keep your characters per line to 65 or less. This works well to stay within most computer screens. Also by keeping your characters to 65 or less you will be able to stay within your 2-page guideline for your newsletter.

A good way to keep your newsletter simple is type your newsletter out in a word processor (I use Microsoft Word 6.0). From within the word processor I check the spelling with the spelling checker and the grammar, and then I save it as text. By sending your newsletter as "text-only" you ensure that not only can you reach the widest possible online subscribers, but that your subscribers will see your message the way you sent it.

Don't get too fancy adding logos or graphics to your newsletter. Why? So anyone anywhere with any e-mail program can read your newsletter. Since you may never have the opportunity to meet your subscribers in person, your Newsletter will project your image. Without a doubt you will want your newsletter to look good on the screen of each and every person receiving your newsletter.

To accommodate the widest range of e-mail programs, you need to limit the length of each line in your newsletter to 65 characters and use a hard line break at the end of each line. You can create a hard line break by pressing the ENTER key. Look at the example below. Limiting your line length to 65 characters and using hard line breaks will prevent most e-mail formatting problems. Without hard line breaks, your newsletter will wrap in places that you had not expected and your message might look like the one illustrated below

This is an example that did not use hard line breaks with their newsletter but relied
on a word wrapping feature to end each line. In this example the newsletter may look just
fine in your text editor but your subscribers get a newsletter that looks something like this.

Be professional and look professional. Never send out a newsletter without checking these items first.

Do You Need A Text Editor?

If you do not have a text editor, go to *http://www.download.com* and search for text editors. Type "text editor" in the search box and you will get a list of available text editors, both freeware and shareware. Don't know which one to choose? Start by checking a FREE text editor called "Super NoteTab Light." If you are looking for a text editor with all the bells and whistles, check Textpad at *http://www.textpad.com/* Textpad is a shareware program. You can download a trial copy at the Textpad site.

Sample Newsletter

NEWSLETTER TITLE
Description of Newsletter
Date Issue #1
Your Name, Editor, johndoe@yourcompany.com

By subscription only! Welcome to your next issue of
"YOUR NEWSLETTER TITLE HERE".
You are receiving this newsletter because you requested a subscription. Unsubscribe instructions are at the end of this newsletter.

IN THIS ISSUE

> *Sponsorship Notice*
> *Feature Article*
> *Industry News*
> *Review of Products or Services*
> *The Spotlight*
> *Feedback from visitors*
> *Guest Column*

> *Classified Ads*
> *How to Be Featured as our Guest Author*
> *Subscribe/Unsubscribe information*

SPONSOR NOTICE

If you have a sponsor, you will place the sponsor's advertisement right here.

FEATURE ARTICLE

Start the first paragraph here. To keep the formatting of the page easy to read, leave 2 blank lines before you start the next paragraph.

Start the second paragraph here.

COMPANY NEWS
Author's Name, Title

Start the first paragraph here. To keep the formatting of the page easy to read, leave 2 blank lines before you start the next paragraph.

Start the second paragraph here. Keep the width of the Document to 65 characters or less. End each line with Hard return (press ENTER).

_____-Tip of the Week_____-
This is a good place for an exciting tip that won't take up a lot of space Make it short and sweet!
_____-Tip of the Week_____-

REVIEW: Products or Services

Start the review here. Use consistent formatting.

SPOTLIGHT: on
Byline, title

From our Readers:

Start Subscribers comments here.

GUEST Column
Byline, title

[Article goes here]
Article goes here
# # #

[After each guest article identify the writer, how to reach them, web site]

How to be a guest columnist instructions

CLASSIFIED ADS

Ad #1
****

Ad #2
****

Ad #3

Copyright information

Copyright 1998 Your Name Here

List Maintenance:
To subscribe
Subscribe@yourcompanyname.com

To unsubscribe
Unsubscribe@yourcompanyname.com

Online issues can be found at
http://www.yourcompany.com/archives

—————————*Your Signature File*————————-
Your Name
Your Company Name
Your Email Address
Your Address, City, State Zip Phone

Display your privacy policy. Make sure your subscribers know
that there E-mail addresses will not be sold or given away.

Sending Out Your Newsletter

Now you have your newsletter set up and you are ready to send it out. But whom do you send it to? It can be sent out to past, present or future customers. Listen to your customers and give them what they want by asking them to reply by e-mail for products or services that would be beneficial to them. Most small business owners that are on the Internet are looking for ways to make more money, or by making their business easier to operate. If you are one of the fortunate people that have products or services that are related to the items above then you have a good chance of making your business thrive on the Internet because of a large target market that is growing by the thousands daily.

Newsletters are a good way to promote your business. Advertising your newsletter is a good way to get people to subscribe. Are you ready to announce your newsletter and launch a promotion campaign to attract new subscribers? Here are a few places to start.

http://www.e-zinez.com/cgi-bin/hyperseek/directory.cgi

This search engine is used exclusively for Websites publishing Newsletters.

http://www.meer.net/~johnl/e-zine-list/submit.html

Add your newsletter to this newsletter list. The newsletter list is a directory of periodically published newsletters. John Labovitz maintains the Website.

http://www.dominis.com/Zines/

Dominis is the ultimate newsletter database. The last time I checked they had over 3000 listed.

http://scout.cs.wisc.edu/scout/new-list/

If you have a newsletter subscription you would like added to this list please send an email to *Nancy@ezine-news.com* They send a newsletter to everyone that sends them information to add to their Website.

You can use other newsletters to promote your newsletter. Announce your new FREE newsletter; along with subscribe instructions, in the classified ads of newsletters similar to yours. Another great way to attract new subscribers is to write articles and submit them to other newsletters. For a list of several hundred of the best newsletters send an e-mail to *new@yoken.com* the list will be sent back to you via e-mail.

Another way to promote your newsletter and get some FREE advertising in other newsletters is by trading ads with other newsletter publishers. Most smaller e-mail newsletter publishers will be happy to use up extra space they have available. You can increase your subscriber database quickly by doing this. Advertising your newsletter on your Website is another great way to build your subscriber database. For people that contact you via e-mail about your newsletter you will want to get as much contact information as possible. What you should ask for is their Website address if they have one, their e-mail address, their physical address, and their phone number. By getting their Website address you can visit their Website and get an idea of the products or services that they could use. This is a great way to produce new products or services. When you publish your newsletter you will have more content to provide your readers and you didn't have to take the time to decide what your customers are looking for. Keep all of this contact information in your subscriber database (I use Microsoft Access) as my database software.

Distributing Your Newsletter

There are many ways to distribute your newsletter. I will show you several solutions to delivering your newsletter.

You can keep in touch with your newsletter subscribers by using ListBot *http://www.listbot.com* there is no software to download and this fully automated utility can have your list up and running in 15 minutes.

Another Website to check out is Findmail *http://www.findmail.com/info/makelist.html.*

I recently came across this Website. Using his or her service anyone can easily start an e-mail newsletter list just by filling out a form. Although I have never used Findmail it appears to be similar to ListBot and the best part about this utility is that it is FREE. *http://www.sparklist.com*

For the Do-It Yourself

The tasks involved in "do-it-yourself" include capturing email addresses, adding email addresses to your database, removing email addresses from your database and actually sending the e-mail to members of your list. You can send your newsletter by utilizing your e-mail program.

If you have a small list, you can cut and paste and use the BCC field. Make sure you use the BCC field and not the cc (carbon copy) field. The names you put in the cc field are visible to all recipients. By using the BCC (blind carbon copy) field, only the recipient's name will be visible.

You can also use FREE e-mail software programs like Eudora and Eudora Pro *http://www.pegasus.usa.com/* or Pegasus *http://www.pegasus.usa.com/* To send out your newsletters to your subscriber base. *http://www.coloradosoft.com/inbox/index.htm*

Inbox Organizer is for anyone who manages a mailing list, has a web page, or uses e-mail! Inbox Organizer allows you to quickly and easily manage the wealth of information contained in your e-mail Inbox. You can download a free trial version for 30 days from their Website to see if it will work for you.

ColoradoSoft WorldMerge Software
http://www.coloradosoft.com/worldmrg/index.htm

What you can do with WorldMerge? With WorldMerge, you can quickly and easily generate large numbers of personalized e-mail messages using your "Internet-ready" database of recipients and a "template" e-mail message. You can also send unpersonalized or "broadcast" messages to your recipients even faster!

Advertising Your Newsletter

Advertise your newsletter just like you would advertise your products or services. This is less offensive than sending out e-mail ads or sales letters to an unsubscribe list. Spice your newsletter ad up by giving your prospects a look at some of your products. Use your best products and benefits and tell your prospects that those are just a few of the products that are covered in your FREE newsletter.

Here is a good headline that will have your prospects chomping at the bit. "Get your FREE newsletter (a $169.00 value) and see how to use a merchant account to increase your sales by 80%. Limited offer subscribe now!" If you are just getting the word out that you have a new newsletter you can post a message about your recently launched newsletter at *newlist@hypatia.cs.wisc.edu*

Check out Cyber Messengers Website at:

http://www.geocities.com/WallStreet/9611/ let them know that you have just launched a new newsletter and they may include your listing in their newsletter.

http://slife.com/ is a Website that offers a newsletter that gives a list of free things including newsletters. Check them out and submit your newsletter with them.

Lifestyles Publishing *http://www.lifestylespub.com/* offers a unique service that gives you all the information you will need to start, maintain and track a highly effective Internet newsletter (E-Zine) advertising campaign. Lifestyles offers a report, it is called the "Directory of Ezines". The Directory of Ezines gives you a total overview of publication times, ad rates, ad dead lines, number of subscribers and everything else you need to know to advertise in a great number of Internet newsletters. This is a must have report! The cost is $19.95.

You can also submit your newsletter to the media by sending out a press release *http://www.newsbureau.com/* News Bureau will send out your press release to over 2000 media professionals.

Subscriber Courtesy

As a newsletter publisher you should take the steps to maintain the integrity of your subscriber base. Should you choose to correspond to your prospects by the means of a newsletter, you should be perfectly honest with them about what kind of newsletter they are subscribing to. Do not write things that are deceptive that will damage your reputation, tie up your time and technology, and misrepresent any and all people that are directly or indirectly connected with your newsletter.

If you include other businesses and or business people or their products or services in your newsletter, let your subscribers know that what they are selling is on the level. This could hurt your reputation as if they were your own products or services. Let your subscribers know that you never send unsolicited e-mail.

Chapter 22

How To Write A Sales Letter That Will Have People Eating Out Of Your Hand

"Focus on the journey, not the destination.
Joy is found not in finishing an activity, but in doing It."

—Greg Anderson

Congratulations, you have just made it through the two toughest parts in generating sales. Let's review, it started out with writing that killer headline that have gotten your prospects to read your ad. Then you followed that up with some of your major benefits of your product or service in your ad. The 3rd most important item is your sales letter. After you have finished reading this chapter, you will be on your way to making more sales than you ever thought imaginable.

Stop Writing Sales Letters The Hard Way! Here's How To Turn Any Ordinary Company Into A Booming Business...**Instant Sales Letters** will show you how to have a sales letter that will bring your customers to their knees begging to buy your products or services. *http://www.instantsalesletters.com/al/af.cgi?1421*

If you never purchase another product, Instant Sales Letters templates work. I have used them and the orders poured in. Yanik Silverman has a must have product. It is one of the hottest selling products online, and for a good reason. Plus he lets you use them FREE for a year and if your not satisfied that they do everything I say they do, he will gladly return you 100% of your money, no questions asked.

Your potential customers do not care about how many sales you have made. They want to know how you are going to help them and what you can teach them to make them successful. That is one of the benefits I am talking about. The reason someone will read your sales letter is because your headline made a statement. They are curious. So don't drop the ball now. Suck them in with your outstanding sales letter.

The reason you wrote your headline, your ad, and your sales letter was to make sales right! Well that is partly right. Some people will be ready to buy now, and some may not. When you're doing business online you're dealing with a very educated group of people. These people are craving for more information before they decide to buy. There is no possible way you can show them all of the products or services you provide in your sales letter. So your next step is to draw them into your Website. You will do that with your sales letter.

There are a couple of different ways for you to deliver your sales letter. One is to give them an e-mail address that will lead them to an Auto-Responder, which will automatically send them your sales letter. This the same way they received your ad. The other one is to leave your Website address (URL). When they get to your Website you will have a copy of your sales letter at the address you sent them to; i.e.

http://www.wave5marketing.com/salesletter.htm

By doing the two things mentioned above you have just pre-qualified your prospective customer. By using this technique you have used very little of your own time in getting them to read your headline, ad, sales letter, or getting them to your Website. You have just given your prospect all the information you need to in getting them to buy your product or service. If they need more information you have sent them to your Website, which is where you wanted them to go in the first place. With a carefully written sales letter you will be almost guaranteed a sale.

To help you finalize your sales I will show what you need to put into a sales letter. Your sales letter should be an extension of your headline and ad. If you are following up your ad with your sales letter and sending it by e-mail or snail mail (mail by the postal service) and you are not using an auto-responder, it should be sent within 24 hours. The reason is you have a hot prospect and you want make the sale give them all the information while it is still fresh in their mind.

If your prospect requested more information by way of an Auto-Responder or if they contacted you through e-mail you have just attained something that is very valuable, their e-mail address. If you hear nothing from them after 24 hours don't assume that they are not interested, they might just need more time to think about your offer. Wait two or three days and then follow up with a free report. This free report can be a report that details one of your products or services, but put a dollar value on it. For example if you sell informational products, you may have a report that you sell for $10.00 to $20.00 by giving this report to them free they may want to look farther into what you have for sale.

If they still don't respond, don't be pushy. I have made some sales as far long as 6 months later and some people just need more time than others to think about your service do or products do. Bottom line here is consistent follow up usually gets results. In your sales letter offer a guarantee. The bigger the guarantee the more trusting and credible you become. What you want your prospects to think is that with the guarantee you offer there will be little or no risk involved by purchasing your product or service. Whatever it is that you sell you should offer no less than a 90 day 100% money back guarantee. On my products and services I offer a full 1 year 100% money back guarantee. I have also seen guarantees for 5 years. By offering a lengthy guarantee you give your customers the chance to test out your products. I have been thinking of trying a life time guarantee, just as a test to see if it will produce more sales, but as of now it is just a thought.

By offering a short guarantee you may force your customers to hurry through your information and not give them time to test it out. Certainly you can not do this for everything that is sold online or off-line, but when it applies to your product or service don't hold back. You will see a large increase in sales. Just as an example, I purchased a Dodge truck about a 3 years ago when they changed their body styles. It came with a warranty that none of the other automakers offered. The warranty was for 7 years and a 100,000 miles on parts and labor for any thing that would be defective. The first thing that came to my mind was that if they could offer this kind of warranty they must have a lot of faith in the product that they built.

To enhance the value of your product or service throw in a few free items. Like stated earlier put a dollar value on these freebies. For instance as you know when you purchased my home study course you received 3 free reports. That with the amount of money that my course will save you when you follow everything I teach will make the course valued at over $1000.00. Now you can't just say it will, you have to add everything up and explain in detail the savings. Make sure your guarantee stands out and above your competitions. But you have to prove this. So put it in black and white. Sometimes it depends on how you word it. Here is an example:

"Guaranteed to increase sales"
Or
"Guaranteed to increase sales by 33%"

Of course the last statement would be the better guarantee, but as said earlier be prepared to explain how you came about the 33% figure. It is better because it is more detailed and in-depth in how it will benefit your prospects and their business. Offer in your sales letter different ways to pay for your product or service. Give them the option of paying directly from your Website, by credit card, check by fax, phone, or by means from your Website, by calling an 800 number.

Remember that some of your customers may be new to the Internet so give them detailed instructions to make their online shopping a good experience. If they are new in their business venture they may not have a large budget to operate with so offer payments spread out in 3 separate payments. Do this as a last resort. It is best to get all your money up front. By doing this you are expanding your market, and the good news of this will bring you more referrals.

If your product or service sells for say $200.00, you can spread that out over three monthly payments of $66.67. So instead of offering your product or service for $200.00 offer it for $66.67 in three payments. What this does is that it doesn't make it sound so expensive. By offering separate payments my business grew around 20% now this doesn't seem like much, but if you have a large database of customers it can be a huge difference. If the benefits of your product or service are strong and easily seen then the sale can sometimes seem as though it was an impulse buy. An impulse buy requires less effort on your part and that is why we have all this technical software, computers and online business to make things as simple as possible to make a sale.

Bottom line is if you offer a product or service that people want, offer a bonus or something free with high perceived value that is cost effective, offer a compelling guarantee, and multiple payment options. By doing all of the above you have just made your offer irresistible. Do not write off a customer who is not satisfied, they could become your best customer and best source of new customers. When sending a refund also send a questionnaire with the refund. By sending out a questionnaire you can find out why the customer was dissatisfied. Was it the product or service, the delivery time, the cost, or was it a problem with the payment transaction or maybe customer support or follow up. This is just another way to improve your business and increase your sales.

Handle your dissatisfied customers with the same respect and courtesy that you handle your satisfied customers. The reason for this is, you may not have sold them anything this time around, but they may return to your Website at later date and decide it is time buy.

Don't drag your feet when sending back a refund, it should be sent out within 24 hours. If your customers call for customer support, or e-mail you, respond immediately if possible, or at the first possible chance. Check your e-mail and answering machine daily. I like to do it right away in the morning while my mind is still fresh. If I can't get a hold of them I will leave a message or e-mail to let them know I tried contacting them. Every business seems to have to deal with complaints, but the best way to avoid complaints is don't let them happen. Don't give your customers a reason to complain.

When there is a change in your business procedure contact all of your customers. That is one of the reasons why we have a database. This should be done in a timely fashion as well. Doing business over the Internet has made this a breeze. Thanks to different software programs and e-mail. In fact you can use a list server to send the same message to hundreds of people with the click of a button.

http://www.lsoft.com/win95-eval.html

Lsoft is a good site to sign up for a free shareware version of a list server. Do this and see whether or not listserv is for you

http://www.lyris.com/down/

You can download and use Lyris at no cost to create as many mailing lists as you like, with up to 200 members per list. To add more members, you will need to purchase Lyris and activate the larger capacity with a serial number, which they will provide to you. MultiView is included with Lyris.

If you are selling a product or service that saves your customers time and money, included that in your sales letter. For instance, the home study course that I sell costs $197.00. By using everything that I teach will save you money that far exceeds the price of the course. So include the price of your product or service and then state the perceived value.

The last thing I want you to know is that above all, be truthful about your company, your products, or your service. Since the mid eighties people have been exaggerated to in such an extreme way through advertising, that people have become very skeptical about things people or companies say about features and benefits of their products or service. The number one reason is that very few people will be persuaded to buy from you if you tell them something that isn't true. So be honest!!!

Here are three Items that you want to stay away from:

Item 1) Trying to be someone you're not.

By this I mean making your customers or prospects that you are knowledgeable in certain areas by giving them partial or incorrect information.

Item 2) Promises not kept

Promising your customers more than what you can deliver because you want them to perceive you to be more knowledge-able than your competition just to make a sale.

Item 3) Blatant Lies

Lying to deceive your customers into buying something you have no intention of delivering.

The lively hood of your business relies not just on your new customers, but more on repeat customers or those prospects that have been referred by satisfied customers. By being dishonest you will lose the customers you have, there will be no referrals, your business will suffer, and eventually die, so don't go there.

Whatever it is that you sell, if it produces a benefit for a person, and that benefit works for them, then you will have a customer for life. Just by word of mouth you will gain customers that you did not have to advertise to get. In this day and age free advertising is unheard of. But if your customers are not satisfied with what you sell them, then that will come back to haunt you just the same as if you sold them something that made them money or whatever benefit they gained by doing business with you.

THE 2 STEPS TO WRITING A GREAT SALES LETTER

Step #1) The Outline

Every successful business started out with a plan. To write a great sales letter you need to start out with an outline. These are like little sub categories or a rough draft. I will give you the steps and all you have to do is fill in the blanks for you particular business. This is what goes into my outline: I start out with 8 or 10 of my best products or services. If you have less, then pick a few. For each one, I write down what their features are. Then in a separate column I write down what benefits these features give the customer.

Example: Let's say my business is lawn products.

Products Features

1) Grass seed comes in 3 different size packages
2) Fertilizer 1 application
3) Planter 3 settings
4) Hoses 2 lengths
5) Herbicides covers 40 different kinds of weeds
Product Benefits:

1) Grass seed our seed uses 10% less than other seed on the market savings of $55.62 per bag
2) Fertilizer our fertilizer needs no water to become active a will save you $319.11 a year on your water bill.
3) Planter our planter gives you 12 inches more coverage and saves you 60 minutes in planting time.
4) Hoses our hoses have an economy setting that no other hose on the market has, that will save you $103.60 per month on your water bill and we have 2 different lengths that no other company has.

5) *Herbicides covering 40 different weeds with one bag will save you from buying other herbicides that are normally sold in 3 different applications. This saves you time and money.*

Always use figures if you can, as in the first 4 examples. In the last product I listed that you save time and money but I don't say how much. Be specific. Most companies are not.

Your sales letter should tell of how your products or services will produce a benefit or will either save time, money or produce more income or produce a better lifestyle.

Ask your self this, what is it that makes my product or service unique that no other peoples or companies products or service produce? If you can show them something no that no one else has, then you have a product that will most certainly sell and sell big. Remember this if you are developing your own product or service.

Here is an example: you have a lawn mower blade that will cut the grass faster and can save someone 20 minutes cutting his or her lawn. Now this applies to a large number of people who will be a very good seller for you so keep this in mind when developing a product or service. This particular benefit should be the driving force for your lead paragraph. This will be the number one benefit that will keep your prospect interested and eventually will produce the sale. Always plan ahead, you want to be one step ahead of your prospect. Anticipate what might be a reason for them maybe not to buy your product or service and counter with more information or a better benefit but make sure it is honest.

Objection: How come I have never heard of your lawn mower blade?

Response: We are not like Snapper Mowers. We do not spend millions on T.V advertising we use our capital and profits to produce superior products. That why our blade cuts twice as fast.

So when writing your sales letter use short paragraphs and sentences. This keeps your customers interested and even though your sales letter may be 6 to 8 pages long your customer won't think they are in for a marathon reading assignment. Also use words that are simple to understand. A rule of thumb that I use is that if you have to look the word up in the dictionary it is probably a word you shouldn't use. Believe it or not most people have only about a 7th grade reading level. So keep it simple even the most educated people enjoy reading something that is more simple since most of their day is cluttered with complicated things

Be unique in your sales approach. For Instance: Do you spend hours mowing your lawn? Does your lawn mower blade always need sharpening? Do you want to increase your business on the Internet? Find something unusual about your business and incorporate it into your business advertising. Stay away from the I's and focus on the you's. Make your customers visualize what you're selling and how it can help them make money, save them time, or change their lifestyles.

Testimonials are some of the best selling tools available. First ask the customers that have used your products if you can use their names to tell other people just how good your products are. But they have to agree that this is O.K. Use their full name and address and if possible a phone number. First names and a last initial aren't near as effective and it may leave some doubt in you prospects minds.

Free samples or a free report are also a great advertising tool that will pull prospects into a sale. This works great on items that have a value of $20.00 or less but I also use this on high dollar items as well.

Time limits work very well to. On my home study course I have tested different time limits and one that works great is a 1 year or 5 year guarantee. If you have a product that helps people save time or money and works great, these are products that people very seldom return. The reason these time limits work is that it gives the person who might just being doing something part time or who may just be a novice the chance to make your product work for them. They don't feel the need to hurry and try something and if it doesn't work return it right away if there was only a 30 or 60 day limit to return it. Make it a 100% money back guarantee. Your prospects will feel that if you offer this that it must be good.

Another time limit method to use is: "Get this offer while supplies last" or "If you buy within the next 10 days pay $40.00 less. These are call to action offers that give your customer the idea that they are getting a great deal. But to keep your customers satisfied and to keep them coming back if they happen to miss the deadline by a day or two sell it to them for the same price. They will feel like they are in the driver's seat.

Give your customers an easy way to order the same way you did on your web page. Whether it is in the form of a credit card, check by phone or fax, by calling an 800 number, or what ever form you choose. Give them all the options to make it as easy as possible to order from you. I have even let the customers use the products I sell on a trial basis they can pay me later, but I insist on a name address and phone number. You'd be surprised on the added interest I get by using this tactic. But the only time I use this is on informational items that cost me little or nothing to produce. By doing this you gain a trust and credibility that will have people buzzing about your business and expertise.

One of these days I am going to try a lifetime guarantee just to see what the response is. That is the great thing about online advertising is that the cost is minimal and this gives you the opportunity to try different ads and sales letters to see what works best.

Remember the three most important words in advertising: **TEST, TEST, and TEST!**

Chapter 23

How to Advertise in Magazines and Newspapers FREE

"A smooth sea never made a skilled mariner."

—English Proverb

Writing a Press Release can be one of the most powerful ways to let the world know that your are in business. The best part of writing a Press Release is that when it is published you are receiving advertising free of charge. You are also giving newspapers and magazines free content so it works out well for both sides. Being a successful businessperson just does not happen over night. Some people just seem to be in the right place at the right time. Now I don't believe that and what ever you have heard you shouldn't either.

Successful people are successful because they are motivated and have done a number of things correctly. That is what this course is teaching you, not to just rely on one means of marketing but to have many in weapons in your marketing arsenal.

I often relate business and sports in the same category. Being a coach of both I think in many ways they mirror each other. If you have two football teams with equal talent and they train the same then when it comes to game time whom wins? The team that has prepared better usually is the winner.

The same can be said in business with all the software tools, books and information available on the Internet. It creates a level playing field for everyone, so the person that is better prepared will be the one who will be successful. But the person that uses all the resources available is going to be the winner.

The press release is one of those tools and a very powerful one at that. Getting your company name and Website out to the public and becoming known to the world is essential to the survival and success of your business. It doesn't matter whether you run a card shop, bookstore, or window washing is your business, if no one knows your out there, or what your business is about, then your chances of selling your product or service is going to be next to impossible.

You may get a few customers by word of mouth from some past customers, or if you have a Website, from search engines you have registered your site with. You have heard of the cliché "If you build it they will come", well people have found out it doesn't work like that in business on the Internet. You can't rely on customers just doing some window shopping to drop in and then expect to run a profitable business by just doing a few marketing techniques.

You have many choices to get your business off the ground. Offer a fantastic service or product. Advertise on Internet classifieds, build a Website and register it with the major search engines, and by all means write a press release and distribute it out to the media. To use all of the marketing tools available would be ideal, but if you are like most people starting out in their own business your operating on a tight budget. So to go with a huge advertising campaign, to start out with would be impossible. That is why using as many free tools such as a press release is possibly the best way to go until you get a good customer base started.

If you are just starting out or if you are a seasoned marketing veteran using as many of these free tools as you can only makes good business sense.

Your press release can be sent out to as many 7000 newspapers, magazines, and other publications. What does this mean to you? It would be like getting to place over 7000 ads absolutely FREE. What I am going to teach you in this part of the course is how to write a press release, and how to get it into the hands of newspaper and magazine editors. Most press releases end up in the trash before the editor gets past the first paragraph. The reason for this is that most people who have never written a press release don't know what editors like to see in a press release. So I took the time to do a little investigating on my own and called up some local area newspapers and chatted with the editors to see what they would like to see when they receive a press release, and here is what I learned:

Rule # 1 Checking With Publishers

This seems to be the largest complaint of the press. After sending them your press release, don't waste their time by calling, faxing or e-mailing them to see if they received your press release.

Rule # 2 Check your Spelling

This is one of the first things that will get your press release trashed. I use Microsoft Word 6.0 when writing a press release because of the features it offers like the spell checker. An editor may over look a few spelling errors if the content is good, but why take the chance. Take an extra ten minutes to check you're spelling, it could mean thousands of dollars in sales. Internet Explorer.4.0 and Netscape Navigator 4.0 also offer spelling checkers. You can download one or both of these for Free.
http://www.microsoft.com/windows/ie/download/default.asp
http://home.netscape.com/download/index.html

Rule # 3 Your First Paragraph

After your headline, this should be your next most important strategy. You should keep it short to keep your prospects interest.

Rule # 4 Short Sentences

Sentences should not exceed 15 words; paragraphs should not exceed 30 words or four typewritten lines

Rule # 5 Subject Line

The subject line should be a reflection of the contents of your press release. For those of you who are sending a press release to a trade show, be sure and put the show in the subject name. If you are using Eudora or Eudora Pro you can filter the press release to the proper mailbox.

Rule # 6 Check your Content

Have your content checked to make sure it is grammatically correct. This ranks right up there with your spelling. Bad grammar means the express elevator to the trash can. By getting the first two rules taken care of, you will dramatically increase your chances of getting your press release read. If you are using any version of Microsoft word go to the tools on your control bar and click on it, spelling and grammar are the first two items listed.

Rule # 7 Contractions and Pronouns

Know the difference between it's and its. Contractions have apostrophes i.e. it's, can't, couldn't. Pronouns do not have them i.e. yours, ours, hers.

Rule # 8 Double-Spaces

Double spaces between sentences are not necessary. Your browse will not show double spaces so no need for the little extra work. Save your fingers and the space bar. This used to be the rule of thumb years ago but things have changed, so stick with single spacing.

Rule # 9 Quotation Marks

Be careful how you use quotation marks. If you are paraphrasing someone be sure to use them and use them wisely.

Rule # 10 International Spelling

When you are sending your press release abroad, remember to check your spelling, depending on what country you are sending the press release to. Just for an example in the United States this is the way we spell "Favorite" In England they spell it "Favourite". This is common courtesy and editors in other countries will respect you for it.

Rule # 11 Pluralization

Watch your pluralization for correct punctuation. "These trees" not "These Tree's" also remember your possessive statements 'two years' duty' Not 'two years duty'

Rule # 12 Vague Words

By this I mean words like Fantastic, Far Out, Awesome, Humongus.

You want to use words that describe your product without being flamboyant. That is reason that I like to use Microsoft Word. If you go to the control bar and click on "Thesaurus" you can find words of similar or same meaning, but don't go overboard.

Rule # 13 Unfamiliar Words

These are those 100 letter words that some people think makes them look intelligent, but is very hard for the general public to understand. So keep the words small but creative.

Rule # 14 Over use of Words

A definite pet peeve with most editors. If you think that you have a word that really drives your point home, by all means use it but not to the point that you use it in every sentence

Rule # 15 Exclamation Points

Don't use exclamation points after every sentence, or four or five of them at the end of a sentence. Editors know when you are excited about your content. Don't treat them like a novice, they are experts and will pick up on your over used punctuation.

Rule # 16 Your First Paragraph

After your headline, this should be your next most important strategy. You should keep it short to keep your prospects interest.

Rule # 17 New Products and Services

Sending a press release about a new product, new service or new company that maybe will be released in a couple of months, without a Website to look at, or a start up company with big expectations and no information to back them up.

Rule # 18 Knowledge of Your Product or Service

If an editor or sub editor should call you to ask for a little more information know your product or service. Don't read a pitch, editors will see right through that and you may lose your chance to get your release published.

Rule # 19 Vague Press Releases

Editors receive hundreds of press releases daily. If yours are too long or vague and do not seem to apply to their publication, it will not be used.

Rule # 20 Your Target Market

You send a press release to a publication without knowing the audience or what the publication is all about. Later I will give you a list of publications you can use that will help you determine what lists you might want to send your release to.

Rule # 21 Zipped Files

Don't send a word document as a zipped file that the editor needs to download, unzip or read into their word processor. Determine the compatibility, and print of the document you are sending.

Rule # 22 Contact Information

Check to make sure your press releases have a contact name, telephone number, fax number, e-mail address, company name, and product name. If are using it for a trade show is sure to include the booth number. Many companies do not include their reply address so make sure to include that also. Keep it short and to the point.

Rule # 23 How Often to Send Your Release

Don't expect every press release you send to be written-up. It may take time and persistence to make the news. Send press releases regularly, every two months, every month or every week, budget permitting.

Sample Press Release

The following sample press release is in the format suggested for use with the media. In this simple-to-use format, you can input your information and send it to the media.

MEDIA ADVISORY

Headline here: (e.g.: Author John Doe Signs New Book at Doe Books)
WHAT: (e.g.: Book signing at Doe Books by nationally-known author, John Doe, whose new book on Internet Business, BIZ Book, has been published by The Publishing House).
WHO: (e.g.: John Doe, a nationally-known author from Your Town, USA. Previous titles to his credit include Anybook, Yourbook and Ourbook).
WHEN: (e.g.: 7:00 p.m. on Monday, Oct 26, 1998).
WHERE: (e.g.: Your Business at 0000 Your Street Your town, USA).
COST: (e.g.: $0.00).
BACKGROUND: (e.g.: There are more than 55 million Internet users worldwide. The World Wide Web is the fastest-growing portion of the Internet and it's doubling every 12 months. In John Doe's new book, Bizbook, readers will learn how to make this cutting-edge medium a vital part of their lives and business success.

Questions answered include how to surf the technical maze of Internet jargon, how to use the World Wide Web as a profit center and why you need a Web site even if your business is not "commercial."

CONTACT: your name; phone number; e-mail:

To assist you further, there are utilities out on the Internet that will automate how you send out your press release and save you a huge amount of time. By typing out one press release you can send it out to 4000 newspapers and publications with the touch of one button. Here some sites that you should check out before you send out your Press Release:

http://www.gapent.com/pr/

Send press releases to over 7,600 personalized publication contacts (not merely "editor")! Now in 37 countries! You identify the industry, and write the press release. Or, we they write it for you.

http://newsbureau.com/

If you are looking to inform the online community as well as the off-line community of your business by press release then the Internet News Bureau is the place to go. They will send your press release out to Internet and computer magazines; e-zines, e-mail newsletters and online news sources; major daily newspapers; television and radio. With the INB Global List, releases are distributed to the personal e-mail addresses of 1200+ media professionals who subscribe to receive Web-related material for $225.00.

http://www.xpresspress.com/

Global Distribution generally reaches between 800-2500 contacts and is appropriate for a wide variety of our clients.

The typical release includes broad-based business news from public companies' computer and IT news, entertainment industry and consumer entertainment news, Internet business and high-quality, high-interest web event, site and developer news.

Media reach extends to all on-line media, print media (including daily newspapers, magazines and newsletters), broadcast television and radio producers.

http://www.ping.at/gugerell/media/index.htm

This is one of the best places to find e-mail addresses for sending your press release to. You can also download all of the e-mail addresses; they take up about 40 K.

http://www.netextensions1.com/cgi/mem2.cgi?000098-000001

Now you can have your press release distributed instantly via e-mail to over 5400 important members of the media community, including individual writers, tech reporters, editors, broadcasters, freelancers, and press professionals. The cost for Netextensions to distribute your press release to 5400+ journalists and publications is $249 per release.

Chapter 24

Writing Articles For Publications & Free Advertising

"The difference between the impossible and the possible lies in a persons determination."

—Tommy Lasorda (major league manager)

Have you ever wondered who writes all these articles that you have seen in the thousands of magazines that are published and bought daily? Most of the major publications do have a large staff of writers, but even the large magazines look to outside sources for content.

I have watched the Internet grow in the three years that I have been online. I have been doing business on line. I have seen new magazines pop into existence, and I have read their content. So where are these new publications getting the articles that they publish in their magazines? Some of the articles are coming from people like you and me. These writers are ordinary people that I have talked with and discussed business with in online Chatrooms, through e-mail, and through discussion groups. So you're asking yourself, what is the point? You can be a part of this growing number that are using this chance to get some free advertising and gain credibility among our peers. So what does writing an article have to do with free advertising?

Let me take a few steps back and explain how all this works. Magazine editors are always looking for new and fresh content to pass on to their subscribers. You can help by offering articles that you have written for your classified ads, or for your newsletters, or articles that you have posted in discussion groups.

If the content is good (don't under estimate yourself) and it is well written and you offer it for free, these editors will jump at the chance to publish your articles. Once you establish yourself as somewhat of an expert on certain topics the editor will be calling you and asking if you would be interested in writing more articles. You see everyone likes to be able to get things for free and magazine editors are no different. If they can get free content and it is something that their readers like, well you get the picture now. In the end it saves them time and money. So this article that you are literally giving away, How will you get free advertising out of it? Let me give you an example. Let's say that you have written an article about " How to make a Angelfood cake in 5 minutes" You then submitted it to the world-renowned magazine "Cakes and More" and they published the article. At the end of the article you put your contact information. Your name, your company name, your Website address, e-mail address, your physical address, and your phone number.

OK you have sparked the readers' interest and they try your recipe. It works out just as you explained in the article. Believe me then when I tell you that there are a couple of things those readers will do. They will continue to subscribe to that magazine and look for more of your articles. That is exactly what the editor was hoping for. They will pass on this information to their friends and family, who in turn will purchase the magazine as well. By leaving your Website address, it will give the readers a chance to visit your Website. When they visit your Website they will see that you have over 1000 recipes. Wow isn't this great over 1000 recipes. Since I am always looking for new recipes I ask my visitors to send me any recipes that they feel are good. If it is a recipe that I add to my Website they could be eligible for a free drawing of one of my famous "1001 Recipe Book" So now you see where a one or two page article can lead.

Your asking where does the free advertising come in? By having articles published in a magazine, let's say it was a two-page article. You have just gotten yourself a full two-page ad. The costs to you FREE. Lets look to see what a full two-page ad would have cost you. Depending on the magazine, it could have cost you between $1000.00- $4,000.00 per page.

Another great place to submit articles in are the E-zines (Electronic Magazines). What you want to do is find as many E-zines that are related to what your article is about. E-zine owners are also looking for new content and they will let you place links to your Website and your e-mail address in the article in exchange you let them publish your article. The great thing about this method is that you can place the article in thousands of different E-zines. When you do this you can have thousands of people reading your article and then visit your Website for more information on other products or services that you provide. Again all of this exposure is FREE. To find the sites of these E-zines you can search for them by keyword, depending on what your article that you want published is related to. For instance the keyword I would have used for the fictitious Recipe

site would have been "Angel Food Cake" or "baking" The site to find these E-zines is:
http://www.meer.net/~johnl/e-zine-list/keywords/

I strongly suggest that you try this because of the outstanding impact it can have on your Internet Marketing Business and the amazing results it creates.

Check out this site for another list of free e-zines:
http://yoken.com/freeezinelist.htm

Not sure if writing is one of your skills, Here is a great book to teach you all the basics and more. To order these powerful books online go to:
http://www.topfloor.com/techwr/

Making Money in Technical Writing
Turn Your Writing Skills into $100,000 A Year
By Peter Kent. Published by ARCO

Chapter 25

Starting Your Own Business

*"Opportunities are often missed because
we are broadcasting when we should be listening."*

—Author Unknown

Many people have different reasons for starting a new business. Whether it is complete freedom, unlimited opportunity, corporate downsizing, more time for your family, or a number of other reasons. You are joining an every growing list of people that are looking at or have already started a home based business. There have been surveys taken and the consensus is that by the year 2005, of all the businesses in the U.S., 60 % of those will be home based business. The art of estimating how many are online throughout the world is an inexact one at best. Surveys abound, using all sorts of measurement parameters. However, from observing many of the published surveys over the last two years, here is an 'educated guess' as to how many are online worldwide as of September 1998. And the number is 147 million.

The number of people buying on the Web is expected to increase from 18 million in December 1997 to 128 million in 2002, representing more than USD 400 billion worth of e-commerce transactions. By studying these surveys it is obvious that if you have a business that sells products or services you definitely need a web presence if you want to compete with your competition.

What is All the Hype?

How many times have you heard that "a Web Site is a Billboard on the Information Superhighway"? It's not, and treating it as such is a sure way to waste time and lose money. There are two main reasons that Web sites are not like billboards. First, a real-world billboard can be seen by anyone driving by. But nobody will drive by your Web site unless you invite them. Your Web site will be on a computer's hard disk connected to the Internet accessible to anyone who requests to see it. But if nobody requests it, nobody sees it.

The second reason Websites are not billboards is that they can be so much more. A billboard provides one-way information flow; the person passing the billboard reads the message and views the pictures. But a Web site can and should provide a two-way flow of information. Visitors to your site can read your message, but they can also provide you with information. One of the most important pieces of information a visitor to your site can provide is an e-mail address; no I'm talking about asking for e-mail addresses. If people are interested in what you have to say, and if you ask for an address in the right way, people will provide their addresses.

A Website has to be more than just a Website. E-mail is essential to any worthwhile Web campaign. There are a number of ways you can work with e-mail in conjunction with your Website.

Set up Autoresponders

People who send messages to you will get an automatic response, and if you have a good Auto-Responder you can also save the name and e-mail address of each person in a log file.

Electronic newsletters can be distributed via e-mail, to people who sign up by sending an e-mail message to you, or who sign up at your Web site.

You can collect e-mail addresses at your site and use them to send out product announcements, information about changes made to your site, special offers, and so

This is just a very small sampling of what you will learn in this home study course. There might be just a few things in this course that you may be able to benefit from, or you may get use out of every chapter depending on your knowledge of the Internet. What ever the case may be, by using the information in the course you will have the opportunity to reach more people and make more money than you ever dreamed possible. That is why along with the knowledge I offered you a 100% 1-year money back guarantee. If you are wondering how I can offer such an outstanding guarantee, I know all of the secrets, tricks, and information from my own personal experience will make you a ton of money.

10 Nasty Pitfalls to Avoid

1) Running Errands & Traveling

Always plan ahead (this will help you avoid pitfall # 2). Arrange your schedule in order of importance and needs. Make only one trip or as few as necessary. If you make a list during the day for things to pick up on the following day you will be able to combine tasks and trips. Know what you need and who has it (phone, fax or e-mail ahead, if suitable). Find a good time to get it. Notify them, so they can be prepare your order then you won't have to wait. Avoid heavy traffic times like rush hour (including on the Internet).

2) Rushing

If you avoid pitfall # 1 then you won't forget, now you must hurry…but something important just came up (one of those last minute things). Don't try to do everything at once or wait until the last minute. List your tasks and the time it takes to do them. Schedule and plan ahead but allow for the unforeseen. Avoid the costly mistakes and oversights of rushing. If you slow down, think about what you have to do, take your time, and relax you can usually accomplish your tasks and get them done right the first time.

3) Office work, Letters, Reports & Notes

Have a purpose for writing. Keep it short if it is applicable. Get to the point immediately and be clear about it. Avoid unnecessary writing and duplications. Screen all incoming paperwork carefully. Always eliminate that which is of no use to you, but be careful. Keep everything where it can be easily found, updated and applied If you have to keep an inventory of things and where to find it then do it.

4) Meetings

What is the meeting for? What are the subjects being covered? Schedule meetings carefully giving the time date, whereabouts, extent, type, and who is attending. Address the issues. Prepare everyone. Avoid uncalled-for meetings.

5) Radio & Television

Informed viewer or couch potato? What are you watching or listening to? Decide what's really important to you. You can always tape or videotape or listen and watch the rerun. ALTER-NATIVES: Be a self-starter, find hobbies, exercise, read a book, or do something productive. Just stay away from the radio or TV unless you can benefit from the program or show

6) Excuses and Procrastination

Don't start things that you can't finish. Reach your goals & objectives By continually working toward them. Don't put off things that you can do for today for tomorrow! Don't make things harder than what they appear to be. Definitely don't wait until the last minute.

7) Planning & Decision Making

This a cliché that is very true "No one plans to fail, they just fail to plan." But this can lead to the typical "paralysis-by-analysis". To accomplish what you want, you must take the necessary steps. Draw together all the facts. Look at it from every angle Plan it out in detail ahead of time. Combine tasks. Delegate. Prioritize. Last but not least, always get the job done.

8) Computer

What is the purpose of using a computer? What's available-why makes? Reentry's or overlook existing data? If you have a plan then you will know what you need and where & how to get it. Back it ups and prepare yourself for the unexpected. Things like hard drive crashes, and accidentally deleting items. Limit your time online, it can become uncontrollable. Keep a record of it, using bookmarks to save information on Websites. Get what you need and log off. Avoid excessive game playing or unrelated chatting. The computer is a productive tool that should be used wisely.

9) Telephone, Mail & E-mail

Why are you calling/writing or typing an e-mail? Clearly outline what your purpose is and what you want to achieve, exactly whom you are addressing, and the best means of getting what you want. Prepare a brief phone script, or a rough draft of what you want to say or type. After it is complete make sure to double check for errors. Be as professional as possible, remember this is your business.

Don't waste your time. Set a specific time to call write or e-mail your prospects or customers. Take and return all calls, mail or e-mail as soon as possible. Screen calls with an answering device or your e-mail with a filtering device. Give out your phone number, physical address, and e-mail address only to those you want contacting you. When you accomplish your goal or objective move on to the next task at hand.

10) Be Selective

Don't commit to more than you can handle. Be honest with people (and yourself) about what you can take on and they will respect you for it. Use your time wisely. Schedule your day accordingly and know what needs to be done and the time it takes to do it. Decide what are the things that are more important. If you can delegate things out do it, don't try to be superman and do everything for yourself. If you can't fit something into your schedule, no matter how tempting, do accept it! If you can't finish it you will not only hurt yourself but your business and the business of others.

http://www.businessknowhow.com/bkhstartup.htm

The number of people buying on the Web is expected to increase from 18 million in December 1997 to 128 million in 2002, representing more than USD 400 billion worth of e-commerce transactions. By studying these surveys it is obvious that if you have a business that sells products or services you definitely need a web presence if you want to compete with your competition. When you are starting a business it helps to know who your target market might be. Here are a couple of Websites to visit to help you decide:

http://www.headcount.com/help.htm

The purpose of Headcount.com is to provide the viewer with succinct data on the size of specific Internet markets.

http://www.zdnet.com/yil/content/mag/9809/www_2000.html

http://www.nua.ie/surveys/

Chapter 26

Office Equipment

"Some folks go through life pleased that the glass is half full.
Others spend a lifetime lamenting that it is half-empty. The truth is:
There is a glass with a certain volume of liquid in it.
From there, it is up to you!"

—Dr. James S. Vuocolo

Computers

Before you start your business you should run a checklist of tools you will need. A good computer is probably the most important tool you will use. Personally I look at a large number of Websites for future reference so I need a computer with a ton of hard drive space. If you plan on book marking a lot of Websites or plan on producing Websites with a good number of graphics I would suggest that you purchase a computer with a large hard drive. By large hard drive I suggest something over 6 Gigabytes.

As the Internet grows you will be seeing advertising on the Internet just as you do on television. I also need a computer that would help me move from Website to Website as quickly as possible so I went with a 400 MHz processor.

I still do a lot of work with my old 75 MHz Packard Bell that I purchased about 3 years ago, so don't think that you automatically have to go out and buy the biggest and best computer, start out small.

Modems

If you are working out of your home or office you will need good modem to go with your computer. I currently have a 56K U.S. Robotics. I have tried others but U.S. Robotics seems to be the easiest to operate with minimal problems. You can boost your 56K modem up to 90K by going to this Website

Printers

A good printer is a must and most computers come with a bubble jet printer my Packard Bell came with a Canon printer that did just about everything that I needed it to do when I first started out. If you plan on printing out a lot of literature and it includes graphics then I suggest that you purchase a laser printer. Laser printers are more expensive but if you do a lot of publishing it sure beats the bubble jet printers or running down to a printing or copying company like Kinkos.

Like I stated in the previous chapter I print a lot of documents which means I go through a ton of ink. I came across a Website that sells printing supplies at very low price. You can order your printing supplies from Netwares and Specialties at *http://www.net-wares.com/* or call them at **1-800-547-1585**. Just to get an idea how much you can save, I purchased 2 bottles of ink from them and it lasted me 9 months all for the low price of $29.00.

The price of ink cartridges for my printer is about $32.00. For the amount of printing that I do 1 cartridge would have lasted me about three months, so I would have spent around $100.00 for ink from a store like Best Buy which is probably one of the more lower priced stores.

R.E.A.L. Associates is another printing supply company that I ran across that seems to have some great prices, but I have not used their services. Check them out for yourself at *http://www.freeyellow.com/members2/realassociates/*

Or you can phone them toll free at **1-888-819-0038** or use their fax number at **860-229-9752.**

Filing Cabinets

I have found that a filing cabinet with hanging folders works great. There are some things that I like to keep in my filing cabinet instead of on my computer. There are certain documents that I fax out and I keep those on file. I have all my folders labeled so it only takes me seconds to find and fax them. That is just one example, but trust me a filing cabinet will save valuable time.

Fax Machine

Most of the clients that I do business with use computers but their are still a large numbers of businesses that are not online. That is one of the reasons that I have a fax machine. The other reason I have a fax machine because of a utility that I refer to as F.O.D. (Fax on Demand).

What is Fax on Demand

Fax on Demand is a system that allows any caller with a touch-tone telephone and a fax machine to request printed documents and other information 24-hours a day, 7 days a week. Virtually every business has a fax machine, making fax-on-demand the ideal medium for getting your information into their hands. Below are a few ways to use a Fax on Demand system.

Product or Service Cost

Instead of mailing new copies of your price list out every time you make a change, let your customers get the latest price list themselves by offering Fax on Demand. If you like, you can make this document hidden from non-customers by leaving it off the catalog system.

Product or Service Information

How about putting all your product literature on-line, making it possible for callers to request the items they want, when they want them? It will save you time and money, and will get information into the hands of your prospects faster. This is another great way to put your business on autopilot and free yourself up for other important things like marketing your business.

Here are some Websites that offer F.O.D.
http://www.owt.com/businesslinks/fod.htm

One World Telecommunications offers a Fax on Demand system for $16.58 per month for 10 pages and you don't even need a fax machine.
http://www.amscomputer.com/fax.htm

Ams computer services offers one of the most reasonable rates on the Internet for a fax on demand system. For $5.00 per month you can have up to 10 documents available for your prospects to access 24 hours a day 7 days a week.
http://www.tssolutions.com/fod.htm

Total Success Solutions offers the same service, for 10 documents the cost is $15.00 per month.
http://cleese.nas.com/~westg/BizOp/FOD.html

Network Access Services offers a FREE 2 month trial to their fax on demand system, then the rate is $19.95 per month for 2 pages and $3.95 for each additional page. If you are not sure if you want to use this I suggest you try the free trial offer first.

If you are located outside the United States then you will want to visit this site: *http://www.netlink.co.uk/users/euromktg/ema/tele-com/FOD.html* Their prices are a little higher, but then I think that may be because it is in Europe. You can try theirs now by using the handset on your fax machine to call **(44)(0) 1923—682600**, and ask for document **362**.

Should you have more Than 1 Phone Line?

I personally use 3 separate phone lines. One for my computer, a dedicated line for my fax machine, and a separate one for my business phones. If you are running your business online it is very helpful to have your phone line free to be able to receive phone calls coming in as you work online, as well to be able to receive faxes while you are using your other two lines. A telephone headset also comes in handy while your hands are busy typing. I recently read about a service that uses one 800 number for all of your other numbers.
http://www.ag-online.com/esa/sob/esafeatures/index.htm

For around $30.00 per month you can get options that when your customers call they will never get a busy signal. The call can be forwarded to any number you choose, whether it is your cell phone, pager mobile phone, or even your business phone. It can call these numbers separately or all at the same time. *http://www.internetcallmanager.com/*

Internet Call Manager is a type of software that you download on your computer and it lets you know when you have a call coming in and if you want to take the call or have it forwarded to another number such as a pager or cellular number. By going to their Website you can download a trial version and check it out.

Working Out Of Your Home

If you are working out of your home keep the office part of your business separate from the living area of your home. If you are building an office area in your home insulate it well to keep out the household noise at a minimum, so there are no interruptions when you are conducting business over the phone.

Surge Protectors

Don't be without a good surge protector. Last April I had a modem ruined by a lightning storm so a surge protector that you hook your computer and phone line is a must.

Setting Your Office Up

Your home office should reflect your spirit. It is important to keep an organized space that feels great to come to everyday. I look forward to come to my office everyday because of the atmosphere that I have given to it. I have surrounded myself with things that I like. I have great stereo system and daylight windows that make the office more like a place that I want to come to.

By having my office set up the way I want it, I feel relaxed and my customers say it shows just by the way I talk on the phone to them. For me going into business for myself has been the best thing that has ever happened to me. Can you say that about your job?

Need help setting up your office? I happen to know an excellent person to help you organize your office to keep you running things as efficiently as possible. LaDonna Wieland has all the tools necessary to make sure look professional and impress your clients. You can e-mail her at *offorgnzer@aol.com*. She'll be glad to assist you both over the internet or on the phone if your from out of state.

Setting Your Goals

I am a goal-oriented person and I have found it very useful to make a list of my goals and a time span to complete those goals. One thing that I suggest is that you have two sets of goals, long term and short-term goals. Here are 7 positive things that happen when you set goals for yourself.

1. Increased productivity
2. Higher customer satisfaction
3. Greater income
4. More sales
5. Higher profit margins
6. Improved morale
7. Improved relationships

6 Guidelines to Achieving Your Goals

1. When you are making your goals they should be something that you really want not just something you dream about.

2. Make your goals realistic. For example, when I started out with my online business I knew that I would like to have an office full of all of the most modern equipment. I knew that I needed to have at least $5,000.00 in order for this to happen so I figured that if I made 2,500.00 a month that in 4 months I could buy the equipment and still pay my other bills. I didn't go out and buy everything on a $500.00 a month income.

3. Write out our goals for where you want to be not because you have negative thoughts about what you wanted in the past.

4. Be specific about your goals. It is not good enough to say that you just want to have more money, but that by the end of 6 months you would want to make $10,000.00 a month

5. Make sure your goals are high enough but not so high that you can't attain them.

6. This is the most important, write your goals as though you have already accomplished them. "I have sold three hundred copies of my book in 6 months".

We now know how important it is to write down your goals. But you need to do more then simply write down some ideas on a piece of paper. Your goals need to be complete and focused. If you follow the 6 steps I have outlined above you will be well on your way to achieving everything you deserve. Research (Damon Burton, 1983) has shown that people who use goal setting effectively:

1. **Suffer less from stress and anxiety**
2. **Concentrate better**
3. **Show more self-confidence**
4. **Perform better**
5. **Are happier and more satisfied.**

My long-term goals are goals that I want to achieve 6 months and longer. I also have a daily to do list. What I have found out that works well for me is to post my weekly duties at the beginning of the week and prioritize them. What I did was to purchase a white board and erasable colored ink pens. This is where I write down my weekly list. As I complete the tasks I cross them out I don't erase them until the end of the week. The list would include such things as my business meetings, conference calls, or just simple things as running to the Post Office.

I have a monthly calendar on my computer, but I found out early on that unless I have my list of things to do in front of me that there have been things that I missed. This has saved me from missing important meetings, and phone calls. The last thing I do at the end of the day is I take the last 30 minutes to clean up and organize my office. Everything that I have used is put back into place. When I come back to my office the next morning clean and in order and I am ready for another day.

Chapter 27

Organizations to Join

"Great things are only possible with outrageous requests."

—Thea Aleaxander

To stay in touch and expand your business on your local front I suggest you join some of your local organizations.

The Chamber of Commerce is an excellent organization to join. Not only is it a good place to network your business, but you will stay on top of local issues. It is also a good source of new business that is coming into your community.

Your local Rotary Club is another good organization to look into. My local Rotary Club holds luncheons monthly. They are always looking for guest speakers to speak at these luncheons, so if speaking is in your marketing arsenal then by all means contact your local Rotary Club.

If you belong to a local church or religious organization this can also be a good source of new business contacts. The thing that I like most about working with people from my church is the fact that I know and trust them.

If you do any type of community service you are meeting new people and you are giving back to your community things that they have given you. I have coached various sports for my children and I have coached in a midget football organization for the past 7 years.

This has also proven to be just another avenue to network. Lincoln Nebraska has approximately 250,000 people. There is hardly a place that I go that I don't run into someone I know through organizations that I have belonged to. This I have found is one of my best local marketing tools, so don't forget to look out your door.

To get your self or company global recognition join the Association for International Business serving 6,500 members in 150 countries. The membership fee is $30.00 per year.

There are a number of benefits that come with the member ship and the executive director Ray Gabriel offers a full refund if at any time during the year that you feel that you have not gotten your moneys worth.

Chapter 28

Books To Buy

"You create opportunities by asking for them."

—Patty Hansen

Guerrilla Marketing Online: The Entrepreneur's Guide to Earning Profits on the Internet—Jay Conrad Levinson, Charles Rubin; Paperback

Cyberbuck$: Making Money Online
Kim Komando / Paperback / Published 1996
Price: $27.99 ~ You Save: $7.00 (20%)

Cybermarketing: Internet E-Mail CD-ROM Online Services Edi Advertising Market Research Publicity Sales Customer Service and More

Len L. Keeler / Paperback / Published 1995
$19.96 ~ you save: $4.99 (20%)

Cyberwriting: How to Promote Your Product or Service Online
(Without Being Flamed)
Joe Vitale / Paperback / Published 1996
Our Price: $15.16 ~ You Save: $3.79 (20%)

Electronic Marketing
Margo Komenar / Paperback / Published 1996
Our Price: $23.96 ~ You Save: $5.99 (20%)

Guerrilla Marketing Online: The Entrepreneur's Guide to
Earning Profits on the Internet
Jay Conrad Levinson, Charles Rubin / Paperback / Published 1997
Our Price: $11.20 ~ You Save: $2.80 (20%)

Guerrilla Marketing Online Weapons: 100 low-cost, High-
Impact Weapons for Online Profits and Prosperity
Jay Conrad Levinson, Charles Rubin / Paperback / Published 1996
Our Price: $10.36 ~ You Save: $2.59 (20%)

The Internet Marketing Plan: A Practical Handbook for
Creating, Implementing and assessing Your Online Presence
Kim M. Bayne, Kim Bayne / Paperback / Published 1997
Our Price: $31.96 ~ You Save: $7.99 (20%)

Marketing Online: low-cost, High-Yield Strategies for Small
Businesses & Professionals
Marcia Yudkin / Paperback / Published 1995
Our Price: $10.36 ~ You Save: $2.59 (20%)

Marketing Online for Dummies (For Dummies)
Bud Smith, Frank Catalano / Paperback / Published 1998
Our Price: $19.99 ~ You Save: $5.00 (20%)

Marketing Strategies for the Online Industry (Professional Librarian Series)
Fredric B. Saunier / Hardcover / Published 1988
Our Price: $40.00

Marketing Strategies for the Online Industry (Professional Librarian Series)
Fredric B. Saunier / Paperback / Published 1988
Our Price: $30.00

The Microsoft Merchant Server Book: The Webmasters Guide to Building an Online Storefront
Barry S. Wadman, et al / Paperback / Published 1996
Our Price: $39.99 ~ You Save: $10.00 (20%)

Official Online Marketing With Netscape: With Windows & MacIntosh: Build Your Business With the Power of Netscape
Greg Holden / Paperback / Published 1996
Our Price: $27.99 ~ You Save: $7.00 (20%)

The Online Business Atlas: The Best Online Sites, Resources & Services in: Management, Marketing & Promotion, Sales, Entrepreneurial Ventures, inter
Douglas Goldstein, et al / Paperback / Published 1996
Our Price: $19.96 ~ You Save: $4.99 (20%)

Online Market Research: cost-effective Searching of the Internet and Online Databases ~ Ships in 2-3 days

John F. Lescher / Paperback / Published 1995
Our Price: $15.96 ~ You Save: $3.99 (20%)

Business Line Management, Marketing and Administration: The
International Directory of Online Management, Marketing and
Administration Information
Hannah Khayyat / Paperback / Published 1988
Our Price: $195.00 (Special Order)

Global Marketing for the Digital Age: Globalize Your Business
with Digital and Online Technology
Bill Bishop / Hardcover / Published 1998
Our Price: $15.05 ~ You Save: $6.45 (30%) (Not Yet Published—
On Order)

Marketing Strategies for the Online Industry
Hardcover / Published 1988
(Special Order)

Online Customer Care: Applying today's Technology to Achieve
World-Class Customer Interaction
Michael Cusack / Hardcover / Published 1998
Our Price: $36.00 (Back Ordered)

Online Management and Marketing Databases, 1989 (An Aslib
Online Guide)
Angela Haddon (Compiler) / Paperback / Published 1989
Our Price: $39.00 (Special Order)

Online Marketing Handbook, 1998 ed.
Daniel Janal / Unknown Binding / Published 1998
Our Price: $29.95 (Not Yet Published)

Online Marketing Handbook: How to Promote, Adveri
Unknown Binding / Published 1996
Our Price: $72.95 (Special Order)

Strategic marketing for the Digital Age: Grow Your Business
with Online and Digital Technology
Bill Bishop / Hardcover / Published 1996
Our Price: $28.00 (Special Order)

Wholesale-By-Mail Catalog 1996/How Consumers Can Shop by
Mail, Phone, or Online Service: How Consumers Can Shop by
Mail, Phone, or Online Service and
Published 1995

Want to find Check the cheapest books on the Internet check
out these two sites:
http://engine.bottomdollar.com/

The Bottom Dollar Shopping Agent offers a comprehensive,
easy to use, easy to access, and secure way for consumers to
shop the Web by enabling them to quickly & easily compare key
decision factors such as price and availability on an extensive
selection of products from the top Internet merchants.
http://www.acses.com/

Acses checks out price, availability, shipping times and shipping costs of any book at over 25 online stores!
You can order these books at my Website the books are bought
from Amazon the Internet's largest bookstore.

Chapter 29

Legal Issues

"If your gonna win, win graceful. If your gonna love, love faithful.
If your gonna learn, learn by teaching.
If your gonna fall, fall reaching."

—Robert Ellis Oral

First I want to come clean and let you know that I have no legal experience. I do know that there are some legal issues that you should take care of before you start your business whether it is online or off-line. If you are just starting a business that you will conduct over the Internet you need to get in touch with an attorney that has Internet experience. They will be able to give you the necessary advice that pertains to Internet laws.

Your Business Name

If you have decided on a business name, you need to check and make sure that any part or your entire business name hasn't been trademarked. If it has then you must chose another name. Don't wait and think that not everyone will ever see your company name.

Just as an example let's say you use a name that has been requested and trademarked. You have been in business for 2 or 3 years and you have a large client base that has spread world-wide. Suddenly you get a legal notice stating that you infringed on a company legal rights by using their business name or parts of it. They take you to court. Even if they don't bring a lawsuit against you they can make you change your business name. This can lead to way more work than you can ever thought imaginable, not to mention the cost. Not only will you be forced to change your business name, but also you have your name on all your stationery, and business cards. Another thing you will have to change is yellow page ad in the phone book.

Trademark owners have an INDEFINITE amount of time to find, and sue businesses that they feel are infringing on their trade name. You will have to have an attorney that will most likely charge you at least $100.00 per hour if not more. I have seen rates as high as $150.00 per hour depending on where you are located. So you can see where all this can lead. Before any of this happens check your company name to make sure it has not been trademarked and registered before you start business or have anything put in print. If it has not then I suggest you get your business name trademarked and registered.

The price to have a trademark checked is around $150.00, about the same amount that a lawyer would charge you for an hour in court.

Check with your local state and city where your business will reside. They have certain guidelines that you will have to abide by. If your business is operated out of your home make sure that there are no zoning laws that apply.

If you have decided on a company name, Trademark Express offers same day research, FREE attorney consultations, 800 numbers 2 on the West Coast and 1 on the East Coast. Check out their Website at: *http://www.tmexpress.com/*

The cost is $169.00 for a Federal and State search and $169.00 for each country outside of the United States.

You can e-mail them at: E-MAIL: info@tmexpress.com or call them at 1-800-776-0530 or 1-800-550-1520 in California or in Washington DC at 1-800-340-2010

You can also check out your trademark with the U.S. Patent and Trademark Office at *http://www.uspto.gov/*

Do you need an Internet lawyer? Check out these Websites:

http://www.e-preneur.com/legal.html
http://www.business-law.com/Ci/188.html
http://legalnews.findlaw.com/
http://www.virtualrelocation.com/Professional/Legal_Services/

Chapter 30

Closing Chapter

"Dream lofty dreams, and as you dream, so shall you become.
Your vision is the promise of what you shall one day be;
your ideal is the prophecy of what you shall at last unveil."

—James Allen

I want to thank you for purchasing one of the finest home study courses in the world. To better serve you and others in the future please take the time to fill out the survey below and return it by mail in the self addressed envelope that was shipped with your home study course.

Your input is very important to Wave 4 Marketing. It is only because of people like you that make Internet business experience a profitable experience.

_____

_____

_____

1 How do you rate the overall course?

____ Excellent

____ Good

____ Fair

____ Poor

2 What areas did you find most helpful?

_____

_____

_____

3 What didn't you like about the course?

_____

_____

_____

4 What new products would you like to see developed to help your business?

_____

_____

_____

5 Did you receive the course in a timely fashion?

___ Yes

___ No

If your answer was No how many days before you received it after you placed your order?

_____

_____

_____

6 Did you like the packaging and was everything intact?
____ Yes
____ No

If your answer was No, state what shape the course was delivered in.

_____

_____

_____

7 Would you be interested in a Network Marketing Home Study Course?
____ Yes
____ No

8 Would you find it beneficial to learn more about how the tax system can save you money in your small homebased business?
____ Yes
____ No

9 Would you be interested in reselling this Home Study Course for a 30% commission on every referral you send me?
____ Yes
____ No

If you have any further questions or comments please feel free to use the area below.

_____

_____

_____

Whether or not we realize it each one of us has a special gift inside of us waiting to surface! We owe developing these gifts not only to ourselves, but also to those around us as well…The important thing here is not what your gift is as much as that you develop it so you can share it with those around you and in the process further your own personal life! Once we have identified our special talents it doesn't matter whether or not we find immediate success in them, what does matter is that we take a step each day towards our intended goal!

—Josh Hinds